LEGENDARY LIGHTHOUSES
Volume II

LEGENDARY LIGHTHOUSES
Volume II

THE COMPANION TO THE ALL-NEW
PBS TELEVISION SERIES

John Grant and Ray Jones

Guilford, Connecticut

Cover design and maps by M.A. Dubé
Cover photo by © David Moore
Text design by Laura Augustine
Photo credits: pps. ii, 6, 8–9, 11, 13, 16–17, 19, 20–21, 24–25, 32, 36, 40, 42–43, 51, 52–55: Olivia Reeves; pp. v, 2, 4, 18, 26–31, 46–47, 48–49, 146, 148–49, 151–53, 155, 158–59, 160–61, 162, 164, 166–68, 170, 171, 173, 174–75, 176–77, 179, 181, 183, 187, 188–89, 191–94: John Grant; pp. ix, 102, 104–5, 108, 112, 114–15, 117–18, 121–23, 130, 132, 136, 140, 142–45: Lloyd Fales; pp. x, 1, 3, 4–5, 61 (top), 68, 71, 73–74, 75, 77, 80, 82, 84, 86, 88–89, 90, 93, 98, 100: Steve Heiser; p. 12: © Underwood & Underwood/CORBIS; p. 14: © G. Brad Lewis/Photo Resource Hawaii; p. 38: © 2001 David L. Moore; pp. 44, 125, 126: ArtToday; p. 45: © Annie Rogers/Photo Resource Hawaii; pp. 56, 96–97: © 2001 AlaskaStock Images; p. 59: © 2001 Jeff Schultz/AlaskaStock.com; pp. 61(bottom), 63, 99, 101: courtesy of the U.S. Coast Guard; p. 66: courtesy of the Alaska State Library; p. 76: © 2001 Jeff Schultz/ AlaskaStock.com; p. 95: © 1999 Mark Kelley/AlaskaStock.com; pp. 110, 128, 138–39, 172: © Bruce Roberts 2000; p. 178: courtesy of Peter Briant; pp. 184, 186: courtesy of the Rosenberg Library, Galveston, Texas.

The "See It On PBS" logo is a registered trademark of the Public Broadcasting Service and is used with permission.

Library of Congress Cataloging-in-Publication Data is available.

ISBN 0-7627-0953-7

Printed in Canada
First Edition / First Printing

For Joan and Andy
—John Grant

For my editor and friend Laura Strom
—Ray Jones

Contents

Acknowledgments

We owe the United States Coast Guard a special thanks for assisting us in the production of both of the *Legendary Lighthouses* television series and books. We are indebted to them for the many times they were there, whatever the time or location, to provide entry to a lighthouse and for the times they allowed our crews to tag along on their visits to some of the most remote outposts in the country. Like lighthouse keepers of centuries past, the work done by the dedicated men and women of the Coast Guard is much less glamorous and much more dangerous than it appears from afar.

Legendary Lighthouses is also indebted to the hundreds of caring individuals who are taking the lead to preserve the past and ensure the future of America's lighthouses. You'll find many of these folks in the pages of this book. Without their enthusiasm and passion, many lighthouses would be gone or ignored.

The creation of a television series and book such as this is a collaborative effort. There are dozens of camera and audio operators, editors, composers, researchers, and others who are contributors. In particular, producers Jack McDonald, Carolyn Zelle, Steve Heiser, and Lloyd Fales made major additions to the content of the project. The beautiful television images—many of them seen here as small photos—were captured by videographers Frank Swanson, Nick Fisher, and Brett Wood.

PBS provided funding for the television series. Their support has enabled us to document America's lighthouses in ten hours of television programming. Funding for the series was also provided by The Lighthouse Depot. Everyone interested in the preservation of lighthouses is indebted to Lighthouse Depot owner Tim Harrison and his American Lighthouse Foundation.

We owe a debt of gratitude to our television co-production partner, Oregon Public Broadcasting. The series would not be possible without the support of OPB President and General Manager Maynard Orme and Senior Vice President John Lindsay. OPB staffers John Booth and Cheri Arbini made important contributions to the completion of the television series.

I am thankful for having had the opportunity to work with Ray Jones again. Ray is a welcome collaborator and a good friend. This book would likely not be a reality without the early and continued support from Globe Pequot executive editor Laura Strom.

I want to thank all of those people who, for whatever reason, love lighthouses and who have expressed their kind words for the television series and books we have produced.

John Grant
Driftwood Productions

Foreword

Many people dream of one day being able to live in a lighthouse. For most people, lighthouses evoke images of romance, beauty, and nature. Those romantic and alluring associations are valid, but in the past hardship and danger were a daily part of a lighthouse keeper's life, especially at the more remote and isolated stations.

In spite of their physical distance from large populations, keepers were required to maintain the stations in a proper manner, always ready for inspection—cleaning the glass, polishing the brass, painting the tower and other buildings, keeping accurate records, fixing broken equipment, maintaining the fog bell, and, most important, keeping the light shining, regardless of the conditions. When and where they could, they also planted crops and fished to supplement their food because the supply ships were often delayed. Many keepers also planted flowers to help beautify their desolate locations.

As modernization came, automation took over. Lighthouse keepers were no longer needed, and the stations were closed, leaving them exposed to the elements and to vandalism. Only a few stations were maintained and saved. Most, however, were not granted that pardon—they were too remote, too isolated.

But eventually small dedicated groups cropped up to save these historic structures, which are also monuments to the men and women who served at them. These preservation groups soon realized that the passage of time and a lack of funds were their enemies. After being closed up for years, these lighthouses are extremely expensive to restore. And once they are

Built in 1904, the architecturally distinctive **Toledo Harbor Lighthouse** remains active. With its Romanesque arches and bulging round-edged roof, it is a one-of-a-kind architectural gem.

The **Eldred Rock Lighthouse** in Alaska is currently under the watchful eye of dedicated volunteers, who work to maintain this beautiful structure. Alaska, a true maritime state with a very rugged, remote, and harsh environment, needs its lighthouses to keep the traffic on its waterways safe.

restored, they require huge sums of money to maintain. Some help came from *Lighthouse Digest*, a national monthly magazine, which helped draw public attention to the lighthouses and those trying to save them. But time and a lack of money continued to hinder progress.

A small New England group dedicated to saving local lighthouses recognized the need for a national organization to help the smaller lighthouse groups around the country. This recognition resulted in the formation of the American Lighthouse Foundation, a nonprofit organization dedicated not only to saving lighthouses but also to researching and publicizing their history. Since its inception in 1994, through various fund-raising efforts the foundation has begun the task of saving lighthouses whose restoration would be prohibitive for local communities.

Through both the popular PBS television series *Legendary Lighthouses*—underwritten in part by Lighthouse Depot—and accompanying books, additional public attention has been drawn to these lighthouses.

Although some lighthouses are slowly being saved, many more are in imminent danger of being lost forever. Already more than 1,000 of America's lighthouses no longer stand. Without financial assistance many more will share their fate. Once a lighthouse is gone, a vital part of American history can never be replaced. Lighthouses must be saved not only for their beauty, but also for their historical importance.

Only with your help can our legendary lighthouses be saved.

Timothy Harrison, President
    American Lighthouse Foundation
    P.O. Box 889
    Wells, ME 04090

A New Generation of Keepers

Several years ago when we started work on the first PBS *Legendary Lighthouses* television series, we asked ourselves a basic question that guided much of our work. What is it about lighthouses that attracts so many people and evokes such powerful feelings?

Since then we've visited lighthouses throughout the United States, from Maine to Alaska, from Key West to Hawaii, and throughout the Great Lakes. We've spoken to hundreds of people who have some special connection to those lighthouses. As we now complete the story of America's lighthouses with the second *Legendary Lighthouses* series and book, we've learned a lot.

Among other things, we've discovered that these historic structures have an even stronger hold on the American psyche than we had first thought. "For young and old alike, lighthouses seem to have some mystic attraction," says Dick Moehl, president of the Great Lakes Lighthouse Keepers Association. "People have a reverence for them."

Seen as heroic symbols of dutiful self-sacrifice, lonely perseverance, and survival in the face of the earth's most destructive natural forces, lighthouses appeal to nearly everyone.

"To some they are important historical monuments," says Moehl. "To others they are mysterious sentinels that mark the place where the land meets the sea. They have even been compared to dinosaurs."

And much like dinosaurs, lighthouses face possible extinction. We've learned that despite incredible efforts, many documented in this book, lighthouses are in great jeopardy.

Although modern navigational devices have made all but a few lighthouses obsolete, lighthouses are still a prominent part of our coastal landscape, cherished reminders of our rich maritime heritage.

But lighthouses cannot stand for long without willing hands to care for

Legendary Lighthouses videographer Nick Fisher captures some maritime activity at the harbor in Cordova, Alaska.

1

Videographer Frank Swanson and associate producer Amanda Lowthian at work on the *Legendary Lighthouses II* television series at the **Port Isabel Lighthouse** in south Texas.

them. No matter how sturdy their construction, they will eventually crumble and fall for lack of maintenance. Unfortunately conflicting priorities and budget constraints have forced the Coast Guard to automate or deactivate nearly all our nation's lighthouses, and these beacons no longer receive the constant care of full-time government keepers. The venerable light towers have been left at the mercy of time and the elements. Their very survival now depends on the goodwill and hard work of individuals and organizations determined to preserve them.

Happily, wherever we've traveled, *Legendary Lighthouses* crews have found people willing to make the extraordinary efforts and sacrifices necessary to save lighthouses. Their dedication has emerged as a major theme of our PBS documentary series and of this book.

In the chapter on Hawaii, for instance, you will meet Rapp Craig, who set aside his career in the Coast Guard so he could continue to care for the Makapuu Point Lighthouse. Now a Coast Guard reservist, Craig works at an Oahu university by day, but at night and on the weekends he is often at Makapuu Point painting, hammering, and polishing.

"I have worked from top to bottom on this lighthouse, inside and outside," Craig says. "But when I first saw this tower in 1985, it was extremely rusty, had broken windows, and had been vandalized several times." Nowadays Craig keeps the old lighthouse shipshape, and visitors consider it handsomely suited to its spectacular cliffside setting.

Our Alaska chapter will introduce you to people like Dave Benton, whose life has found

Rapp Craig at Hawaii's Makapuu Point Lighthouse

Dave Benton of the Alaska Lighthouse Association

new focus in a lighthouse. Several years ago Benton gave up a high-level position as Alaska's international fisheries negotiator so he could devote more time to the Point Retreat Lighthouse west of Juneau. Led by Benton, the Alaska Lighthouse Association is restoring the light station for use as a museum and monument to the rich maritime history of the Northwest.

"All the stuff we're doing out here is volunteer," says Benton. "Nobody is paid. We've got a core group of about twenty-five folks who come out here for long weekends and work. We put in a lot of hard hours, but we also have a good time."

At the gateway to the Great Lakes—and near the front of our Eastern Great Lakes chapter—you'll find Manny Jerome, who has lived much of his life within sight of the Rock Island Lighthouse. His longtime family summer home is located not far from Rock Island on the banks of the St. Lawrence River. As a boy, Jerome would row across the river to help the lighthouse keeper with odd jobs.

Eventually the Rock Island Station was shut down, and the lighthouse fell onto hard times. About twenty years ago, Jerome decided to lend the old station a hand. "I felt like it was being left for nature to destroy it," he says. "It was time someone did something to preserve the history." Painted and patched, the lighthouse now looks much as it did during its century of active service.

Few light towers in America were ever in more need of assistance than Florida's Cape St. George Lighthouse, which nearly fell into the Gulf of Mexico following Hurricane Opal in 1995. Battered by wind and water and undercut by relentless beach erosion, the

A cameraman films Elmer Harris on his return visit to Alaska's **Cape Hinchinbrook Lighthouse.**

LEGENDARY LIGHTHOUSES II

150-year-old tower developed a pronounced lean. As the tower tottered queasily toward the surf, its plight came to the attention of John Lee, the general manager of a weekly newspaper in Apalachicola, Florida. Together with an innovative local contractor named Bill Grimes, Lee has made a personal crusade of saving Florida's "leaning tower."

"If the right people hadn't been at the right place at the right time, there's no question in my mind that there would no longer be a Cape St. George Lighthouse," says Lee.

Grimes took a number of relatively low-cost, but highly effective steps in his effort to rescue the tower. These included driving 15-foot pilings along the edge of the base and pouring 70 cubic yards of concrete to give the structure additional mass. Apparently, and happily, the rescue effort has succeeded.

Nostalgia alone is not even enough to preserve America's lighthouses into the future. It takes creative thinking. Calvin Byrd, a former mayor of Port Isabel, Texas, made restoring the Point Isabel Lighthouse a priority of his administration. "We were able to get public support by pro-

At times, creating a lighthouse documentary can resemble a safari. Videographer Frank Swanson and audioman Bill Ward look for wildlife near the **St. Marks Lighthouse** in Florida.

moting the project not just as historical preservation but as economic development," Byrd says. "Preserving buildings just because they're old and we like them just isn't enough."

Finding new uses for these old structures is one of the keys to their survival. "We recognize that the lighthouse is not used for navigational purposes anymore," says Byrd. "It's now a beacon of economic opportunity. It's great for the local economy and it's great for community pride."

Legendary Lighthouses is a celebration of the America's lighthouses and of the people who have kept their lights burning—both literally and figuratively—for two centuries. It is also an adventurous journey along some of America's most spectacular coasts. Join us now as we return to the pounding surf and piercing beacons, the intriguing history and dramatic personal accounts that form the story of America's legendary lighthouses.

Enjoy the journey.

The *Legendary Lighthouses* of Alaska television production team relaxes at the remote **Eldred Rock Lighthouse**. Director Steve Heiser, producer Carolyn Zelle, videographer Nick Fisher, and audioman Bill Ward spent nearly three weeks shooting Alaska's often difficult to reach lighthouses.

HAWAII

Jewels of the South Pacific

A Light in the Distance

On June 28, 1927, an ungainly Fokker C-3 Trimotor lumbered down a runway in Oakland, and took to the air. Not long afterward it crossed the California coast and headed out over the Pacific. At the controls was Lester "Lone Eagle" Maitland and by his side was navigator Albert Hegenberger, an MIT-trained engineer. At the age of twenty-eight, Maitland was already a noted aviator. An army lieutenant, he had flown under the command of the legendary General William "Billy" Mitchell during an experimental bombing raid on retired World War I battleships. Some years later Maitland had piloted a small racing plane to a world speed record of 245 miles per hour.

Only the previous month Charles Lindbergh had made his famous flight across the Atlantic. Now Maitland and Hegenberger were attempting a feat no less impressive. They would fly their Fokker, nicknamed "Bird of Paradise," nonstop from California to Hawaii over 2,500 miles of open water. This was an extremely hazardous undertaking, but not just because of the distance. The big tanks on the Fokker held more than enough fuel to make the trip, assuming that Hegenberger's navigating was nearly perfect. But what if it was not? What if their big bird drifted off course and they got lost? Their greatest challenge—and their only route to safety—lay in finding the Hawaiian Islands, which, compared to the vastness of the Pacific, were mere specks on a map.

Their means of navigation was a recently invented radio beacon that Hegenberger had helped design. If all went well, they could lock onto the signal and follow it straight to Wheeler Field on Oahu. But all did not go well. Only a few hours into the flight, something went wrong with the equipment, and their radio receiver fell silent. With no radio beacon to guide them, the two adventurers were faced with a difficult decision. Either they would retreat to the safety of the mainland or press on and put their trust in more traditional navigational skills—not the least of these being their own gut instincts. The aviators decided to keep going.

A day passed and then a night. Starved for sleep, they caught themselves nodding off now and again, but they knew they had to remain vigilant. Bypassing the islands meant almost certain death. There was only empty ocean out there beyond Hawaii.

Kilauea Point Lighthouse silhouetted against the setting sun. The lighthouse is now part of the Kilauea Point National Wildlife Refuge. Visitors who are drawn to the refuge to observe the many exotic birds, are surprised to discover the magnificent lighthouse that marks the most northern end of the inhabited islands.

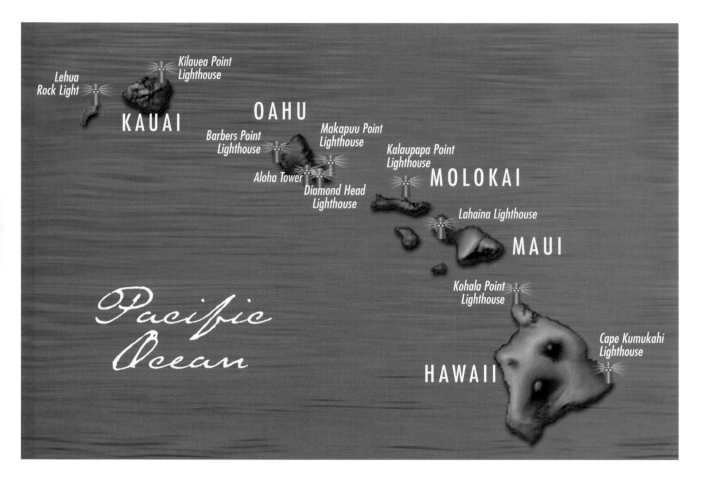

Eventually they would run out of fuel, the Fokker would fall into the water, and, most likely, they would never to be seen or heard from again. They strained their eyes scanning the dark surface of the Pacific for some sign of the islands, but the ocean revealed nothing. As the flight entered its twenty-fourth hour, Hegenberger began to suspect the Fokker had in fact missed its target, perhaps passing to the north and west of the main Hawaiian archipelago.

Then, out of the corner of his eye, Maitland caught a faint glimmer of light. At first unable to identify it, he was faced with a life-or-death decision. He made it without hesitation. Banking the Fokker to the left, Maitland headed straight for the mystery light, and before long its identity became gloriously clear. Its two bright flashes, visible every ten seconds, left no doubt that this was the Kilauea Point Lighthouse, built about fifteen years earlier at the far northeastern corner of the Hawaiian chain.

Kilauea Point Lighthouse overlooks the Pacific from its perch near the top of a cliff, an elevation of more than 200 feet.

Aviators Lester Maitland (left) and Albert Hegenberger several weeks after their history-making flight from California to the Hawaiian Islands. Their adventurous journey might have ended tragically if not for the beacon of the **Kilauea Point Lighthouse.**

Maitland and Hegenberger could now afford to breathe a sigh of relief. It had been a close call. They had indeed drifted off course and missed the Hawaiian chain by nearly 100 miles, far enough to have never seen a hint of land. If not for the Kilauea Point beacon, they would have kept right on flying farther and farther out into the Pacific. But as it turned out, by dawn they were cruising over the islands. A short time afterwards they landed at Wheeler Field on Oahu where both men joyously credited the Kilauea Point Lighthouse with saving their lives.

Having guided several generations of mariners—including, on occasion, the pilots of straying aircraft—the lighthouse is now retired. Today it serves as a key attraction of the Kilauea Point Wildlife Refuge on Hawaii's Kauai Island.

Cyclops of Makapuu

For more than one and a half centuries, lighthouses have been guiding travelers to safety in the Hawaiian Islands. Fewer than 7,000 square miles of land lost in 70 million square miles of ocean, the extraordinarily remote Hawaiian chain has always been a challenge for navigators. Locating the islands in the midst of the earth's greatest and darkest ocean is a daunting task, but one made much easier by the circle of man-made lights that still ring Hawaii like a glowing crown.

The brightest and most powerful of the lights is located at the far eastern end of Oahu, Hawaii's most populous island. For over ninety years, the Makapuu Point Lighthouse has guided mariners in from the immense Pacific and pointed them toward Honolulu's shelter-

On the southeast corner of Oahu, alone and high on a rock ledge, is the first light to mark the way to the important harbor at Honolulu. The **Makapuu Point Lighthouse** is a relatively short thirty-five-foot-tall structure that stands on a ledge some 400 feet above the ocean. Its signal can be seen from ships far to the east of Oahu.

ing harbor. The capital city of Honolulu has long been the primary port of entry for immigrants, tourists, supplies, and imports. Even today this thriving mid-ocean seaport attracts ships and travelers from the U.S. mainland and every seafaring nation. Those approaching from the east may see the Makapuu Point beacon long before they catch sight of the Hawaiian islands themselves.

Thousands of years ago, a series of volcanic eruptions to the east of present day Honolulu poured molten lava directly into the ocean, forming a dramatic escarpment. Much later Polynesian settlers would call this impressive place Makapuu, or "Bulging Eye." Composed of layer upon layer of solidified lava, the nearly vertical walls of Makapuu Point were uninviting to engineers and construction crews. Even so, in 1905 the U.S. Lighthouse Board selected this site for Hawaii's most potent maritime beacon.

Authorities had long recognized the need for a major light to mark the eastern approaches to Oahu and Honolulu. A 1905 report to Congress noted the large quantity of

HAWAII'S VOLCANIC ORIGINS

Beneath the floor of the Pacific lies an ocean of magma. Periodically this molten rock breaks through the earth's crust, generating one of nature's most violent spectacles—a volcanic eruption. In certain places mysterious currents welling up from our planet's superheated interior produce a "hot spot" where volcanoes erupt with great frequency. One such hot spot is located in the mid-Pacific at the southeastern end of the Hawaiian archipelago. Here fluid plumes of magma rise through an intricate network of vents and burst onto the surface as fountains of lava.

Grandest of Hawaii's colossal volcanoes is Mauna Lea, where countless thousands of eruptions have piled up more than 10,000 cubic miles of volcanic rock and ash to a current altitude of some 13,677 feet above sea level. When measured from its base on the sea floor, however, Mauna Lea rises more than 30,000 feet and rivals Mount Everest as the earth's tallest mountain.

Dramatic lava flow in Hawaii

In the past this prodigious mountain-building process has been repeated on each of the Hawaiian Islands, which are, in fact, the peaks of undersea volcanoes. The same hot spot that fuels the nearly continuous eruptions on the Big Island is the creative engine that built all the islands. For at least 70 million years, the hot spot has remained stationary while tectonic forces of inconceivable power have driven the Pacific seabed slowly across it. Volcanoes erupt, are built into mountains of considerable size, and then, as they are shifted off the energizing hot spot, grow cold and extinct. Moving at a rate of a few inches each year, this giant conveyor belt has produced a chain of islands and seamounts more than 3,000 miles long. Even the loftiest of the older volcanoes have long ago eroded to mere stumps with their summits below the ocean surface. Only the main Hawaiian chain and a few smaller islands to the northwest remain above sea level.

Eventually there will be other islands. Already to the southwest of the Big Island a new volcano is rising from the ocean floor. Known as Loihi, it is expected to reach the surface in about 200,000 years.

Perhaps the best place in the world to experience the fascinating phenomenon of volcanism is at Hawaii Volcanoes National Park located on the Big Island. The park offers highly informative tours and a dramatic drive around a seething volcanic caldera.

shipping passing by Makapuu Point. "All deep-sea commerce between Honolulu and Puget Sound, the Pacific Coast of the United States, Mexico and Central America, including Panama, passes Makapuu," said the report. And yet "there is not a single light on the whole northeastern coast of Hawaii to guide ships or warn them of the approach of land." Later that same year Congress appropriated $60,000 for construction of a lighthouse at Makapuu.

Those who built the tower, keeper's dwelling, and storage facilities at this remote light station would discover that Oahu's volcanoes had made no allowance for lighthouses. To level a site crews were forced to blast an artificial ledge from the sheer rock face with dynamite. Then they erected a relatively modest 35-foot-tall tower of stone and steel.

Unlike lighthouses built on low, sandy ground, the Makapuu light tower did not need to be very tall. Its perch on a cliff some 400 feet above the waves provided the elevation necessary for the light to be seen from ships far out at sea. Mariners have often caught sight of it from as much as 28 miles away.

The secret of the Makapuu beacon's long reach is not just its great height, but also the remarkable strength and efficiency of its light-focusing lens. Among the largest of its kind, the Makapuu lens is described as a "hyperradiant Fresnel." Consisting of 1,188 individual glass prisms arranged in an enormous metal frame, the lens compresses light into a single powerful beam that can be seen over great distances. A scatter of French-made Fresnel lenses—first designed by Augustin Fresnel during the early nineteenth century—remain in use along America's coastlines, but none are as large or powerful as the one at Makapuu. More than 8 feet wide, the lens weighs several tons and almost completely fills the lantern room at the top of the tower. Truly it is a bulging eye.

Keeping Up a Bright Tradition

The Makapuu Light Station with its enormous hyperradiant lens first guided mariners in 1909. Ships now had ample warning as they neared the treacherous southeast coast of Oahu. They could guide on the light when approaching the island from the north or the south or when passing through the Kaiwi Channel to the east of the island.

Care and operation of the station was placed in the hands of full-time keepers who lived in a residence a short distance from the tower. The keepers made sure the light was burning each night and took charge of all day-to-day maintenance, such as painting, clean-

Unfortunately, the **Makapuu Point Lighthouse** and its priceless lens have been victims of neglect and wanton vandalism. The hyperradiant lens at Makapuu is among the largest lenses used in any American lighthouse.

ing windows, and polishing the big Fresnel lens. As they went about their duties, keepers could take pleasure in one of the world's greatest views, including the craggy Oahu mountains to the west and a 270-degree sweep of the azure Pacific. In all, three generations of keepers enjoyed this extraordinary scenery while living and working at Makapuu.

At first the Makapuu light was generated by gas lamps. To make sure the lamps burned clean and bright, keepers carefully trimmed the wicks. This task, a common one at nearly all nineteenth- and early twentieth-century light stations, led keepers to call themselves "wickies." Like their fellow wickies at lighthouses elsewhere, those at Makapuu eventually found themselves tending an electric light.

In time not only the gas lamps but the wickies, too, would be gone. As a cost-saving measure, the U.S. Coast Guard began to automate lighthouses along every American coast. Fitted with electronic timers to switch its light on and off without human assistance, the

Makapuu Lighthouse was automated in 1974. That same year, the last official Makapuu keepers packed their bags and left the station.

With the old lighthouse left to stand its nightly vigil alone, it no longer received the daily care and maintenance needed to keep out the wind and rain and protect it from vandals. Although its beacon continued to guide mariners, the station's structures suffered greatly from neglect. Even the lantern room and its priceless Fresnel lens were not exempt. In one especially unfortunate instance of vandalism, a rifleman callously fired into the glasswork.

Then in 1985 the lighthouse acquired a new and important friend. That year a young coast guardsman named Rapp Craig was assigned to complete the annual inspection of the facility. "Makapuu was in very bad shape at that point," says Craig. "It was extremely rusty, had broken windows, and had been vandalized several times."

Seen in stark contrast to the magical beauty of the station's surroundings, the sight of all this damage had a powerful emotional impact on Craig. "I knew from that point on that I wanted to spend a lot of time working here."

Craig was sure the deterioration of the historic lighthouse could—and must be—reversed. "I could see a jewel underneath that just needed to be brought out, polished, and cleaned."

Now in the Coast Guard Reserves, Craig often spends evenings and weekends restoring and maintaining Makapuu, where he has done "Everything from painting to replacing hardware. Just now I'm in the process of restoring the lantern framework," he says. "It's about a third done."

In return for these efforts and his dedication to saving the old lighthouse, the Coast Guard has named Craig the official keeper at Makapuu. Honorary or no, it's a title he relishes. "In actually laying my hands on the lighthouse, I really do feel a connection to all the lighthouse keepers who have been here before me."

Craig also feels a strong personal connection to Hawaii. For him this island state has itself served as a lighthouse. Born and raised in Ohio, Craig joined the Coast Guard while still in his early twenties. No doubt, like most other young recruits, he hoped to travel and spend time on the ocean. Craig served first in California and later on the East Coast. Then in 1985 he was posted to Hawaii.

Makapuu's enormous lens dwarfs Coast Guard reservist Rapp Craig.

"I fell in love with the place," says Craig, "I fell in love with the local culture and the culture of the ocean itself."

In addition to his keen interest in the Makapuu Lighthouse, Craig took to fishing, diving, surfing, and other local water sports. "You just can't do those things in Ohio," he says.

When Craig's Hawaiian tour of duty approached its end, he was faced with a painful decision. To remain on active duty in the Coast Guard, he would have to leave his beloved adopted home. The solution to his dilemma turned out to be the Coast Guard Reserves. He took a job working at a local university but maintained his link with the Coast Guard by serving as a reservist. This arrangement has worked out quite well for Craig, his family, and the Makapuu Lighthouse.

Often, when Craig visits Makapuu Point, he brings his children. "My children have been all over this lighthouse," he says. "They consider it their own. They like to play games here and let their minds wander. Of course, I like it here, too. It's a great place to fish."

But for Craig and his family, Makapuu and its lighthouse represent far more than just fun and games. "It's important for my children to see me working here because it teaches them responsibility," Craig says. "I'm giving them this memory that not very many people can have—of playing up here when their dad was the lighthouse keeper. To do that with my children is just incredible."

The **Makapuu Point Lighthouse** was constructed in 1909 on an artificial ledge that was blasted from Oahu's volcanic rock. Three generations of lightkeepers tended the structure until the Coast Guard automated it in 1974.

Fires on the Horizon

Makapuu and the other navigational lights that now ring the islands are probably not the first navigational beacons to serve Hawaii. It seems likely that early Polynesian mariners who ventured onto the Pacific in outrigger canoes used fires onshore to guide them back to safety. Whether paddling a 20-foot outrigger or piloting a mammoth freighter, navigators have always found Hawaiian waters to be treacherous and unforgiving. Mariners approaching these rocky island shores can use all the help they can get.

Satellite, radio, and radar navigation techniques have become so sophisticated that along most U.S. coasts lighthouse beacons and other navigational lights are now thought to be of only limited usefulness. But not so in Hawaii. Here the lights remain important to both pleasure boaters and commercial shipping.

"The lights still play a vital role for oceangoing traffic in Hawaii," says Craig. "It's one thing to look at a bunch of lines and numbers on a screen, but it's another to look up on a cliff and see a light you recognize."

Hawaii's modern navigational lights are not located on low, indistinguishable headlands as are, for instance, the lighthouses of Florida or those of the Outer Banks of North Carolina. Here lighthouses are positioned on or near the islands' loftiest

Standing at the foot of an extinct volcano, the beautiful **Diamond Head Lighthouse** is one of the last occupied lighthouses in the United States.

and most recognizable seaward features. Interestingly enough, early Polynesian mariners banked their own signal fires in many of these same locations.

Among Hawaii's most famous land-and-sea marks is the volcanic cone and crater at Diamond Head. This extinct volcano a few miles southeast of downtown Honolulu towers above the celebrated beaches of Waikiki. The Hawaiian name for this imposing feature translates into English as "Ring of Fire." While the name certainly seems an appropriate one for a volcano, some believe it refers not to the crater itself, but to the signal fires the Polynesians once lit on this peak to call their canoes home from the sea.

Nowadays another light burns at Diamond Head. Near the foot of the volcano stands the Diamond Head Lighthouse. When the light station here was established in 1899, it was far more isolated than its location near the territorial capital might suggest. At that time, because of the difficult terrain, a journey from Diamond Head to Honolulu could take all day. Today the station overlooks a major coastal traffic artery, placing it barely ten minutes from the center of the city.

Even so, a trip to Diamond Head remains in every sense a journey into the past. The station fairly glistens with spit and polish. It exudes order and efficiency just as it did back during the days of full-time keepers. And it should—for this is the last occupied lighthouse in Hawaii and one of the last anywhere in America.

The beautiful and historic keeper's dwelling at Diamond Head is now the official residence of the Coast Guard's 14th District commander, Admiral Joseph McClelland. Among his other duties, Admiral McClelland commands the Aides to Navigation teams that maintain a modern "ring of fire"—the maritime lights and buoys of Hawaii, Midway Island, Wake Island, American Samoa, Guam, and Sai Pan.

The sun reflected in the Fresnel lens of the **Diamond Head Lighthouse**. "You can't help being affected by the beauty of this place," says Admiral Joseph McClelland, commander of the Coast Guard's 14th District. "I would reckon that it's got to be about the nicest place we have to live."

"It's an enduring Coast Guard responsibility to maintain buoys, fixed aides, navigational lights, and, of course, lighthouses such as this one at Diamond Head," says Admiral McClelland.

The U.S. Coast Guard took over responsibility for America's lighthouses in 1939 on orders of President Franklin Delano Roosevelt, who was preparing the nation for war at the time. Up until then and since the eighteenth century, all U.S. lighthouses and other navigational aides were looked after by the Lighthouse Service, a separate government agency operating under the auspices of the U.S. Treasury Department. Admiral McClelland fits very well into this two-centuries-old service tradition. As the current resident at Diamond Head, he is in spirit, if not in fact, a lighthouse keeper.

Admiral Joseph McClelland, USCG

The Diamond Head tower

"There are people who say lighthouses are obsolete and we don't need them anymore, but that is not the case," says McClelland. "Lighthouses remain important even today in an age of electronic navigation and global positioning systems. The light gives you that gut sense of knowing exactly where you are and where you ought to be."

Technically speaking, as commander of the Pacific-wide 14th District, Admiral McClelland is keeper of not just one, but many lighthouses. Not surprisingly, however, Diamond Head is his favorite. "It's a dear, historic site to many Hawaiians," he says. "And it's a treasure to me and to many others who have been lucky enough to live here."

Like Coast Guard reservist Rapp Craig, Admiral McClelland is proud of his work and relishes his stay in Hawaii. "Certainly to live here is a special privilege," he says. "I spent my sea time on icebreakers, so for an ice sailor to come to Hawaii is a delightful opportunity. You can't help being affected by the beauty of this place—the sun as it moves up from behind the lighthouse in the mornings or the ocean and its changing states from hour to hour."

However, unlike Craig who opted to remain in the islands, the admiral will all too soon be leaving Hawaii. The position of 14th District commander is held by high-ranking Coast Guard officers on a rotating basis, and a new commander moves into the Diamond Head keeper's dwelling every two to three years. "You enjoy it," says Admiral McClelland, "but you always know that you're going to be relieved one day and hand it off to the next fortunate person. You're really only the groundskeeper, the landlord here for a little while. You try to make the absolute best of it you can because you know it's not going to be forever."

As he comes and goes about the Diamond Head Lighthouse each day, Admiral McClelland walks in the footsteps of dozens of Coast Guard officers and Lighthouse Service keepers who lived here before him. From 1899 until 1924, when the light was automated, full-time keepers lived and worked at the station. The light they tended was considered a critical one since it warned mariners away from the deadly shoals lying just offshore and also guided vessels to the commercially vital harbor at Honolulu.

With the relatively limited technology available at the end of the nineteenth century, construction of the station was extremely difficult. "I am continually amazed at the ingenuity, the seamanship, and craftsmanship of the people who built the lighthouses on these rugged coasts," says Admiral McClelland. "And it was all done at a time when we didn't have fancy computers."

Built in 1899, the Diamond Head tower served faithfully until 1917 when severe cracks appeared in its foundation. The damage could not be repaired, so the tower had to be torn down and rebuilt. Given reinforced-concrete walls and fitted with the station's original third-order Fresnel lens, its replacement remains essentially unchanged to this day. Shining out over the Pacific from an elevation of 147 feet, its beacon continues to light the way for vessels headed toward Honolulu Harbor.

Years of Wonder

Diamond Head stands out brightly in the memory of Carol Edgecombe Brown, whose father was the Lighthouse Service district superintendent in the late 1930s. "My family moved to Diamond Head when I was three years old," says Brown. "We had ten wonderful years here."

Even as a child Brown recognized the good fortune of growing up in such spectacular surroundings. "This was a privilege, a real bonus to be able to live here with my family."

For Brown and her two older sisters, the light station was a child's paradise. "I remember playing tag around the base of the lighthouse. We played games, rode bikes, read books, and had many happy meals with friends and relatives. We always had dogs in the yard. And my dad built two tree houses in the magnificent tree at the back of the property."

But the focus of activity at Diamond Head was the lighthouse itself. "It was a never-ending fascination," Brown says. "It was always a treat when we were allowed to go into the tower, where we kind of entered another world. You had the smell of the fresh paint, and I loved stopping at the windows on each side to look out. We would go into the lens room and see the magnificent glass lens up close—that was always part of the ritual. And at the top it seemed very, very high, wide open, and spectacular."

For Carol Brown's father, superintendent Frederick Albert Edgecombe, the light tower was far more than a centerpiece for family activities. It was a constant reminder of his far-flung responsibilities as superintendent of a lighthouse administrative district that spanned the Pacific Ocean. "My dad was in charge of many, many lights," says Brown.

Edgecombe began his career as a civil engineer, not as a lighthouse keeper. Born and raised in Groton, Connecticut, he received his engineering degree from Brown University in 1908. Unable to find steady work, young Edgecombe packed his bags and headed for Hawaii—then more commonly known as the Sandwich Islands. Edgecombe's expertise in construction made him a natural for the Lighthouse Service, at that time building new facilities throughout the rugged volcanic islands. By the 1930s Edgecombe had worked his way up to the position of district superintendent. At that point the Edgecombe family moved into the Diamond Head Lighthouse, which lay at the heart of the district and had been used as a home for superintendents since 1924.

Carol Edgecombe Brown is in awe of Diamond Head's third-order Fresnel lens.

Carol Edgecombe Brown

As it turned out, Edgecombe was destined to be the last civilian lighthouse superintendent in the Pacific. During the 1930s, tensions between the United States and Japan were on the increase, and perhaps in recognition of Hawaii's immense strategic importance, President Roosevelt paid the islands a visit in 1934. Dressed in a white straw hat, Edgecombe stood at the top of Diamond Head Lighthouse to officially greet Roosevelt as the presidential ship approached Honolulu Harbor. Five years later, with war clouds looming on the horizon, Roosevelt abolished the Lighthouse Service, handing its responsibilities over to the Coast Guard.

As many other Lighthouse Service veterans did in 1939, Edgecombe joined the Coast Guard and in this way kept his position as superintendent. But the change in status required

Shortly before the last light of the day fades in the west, the **Diamond Head Lighthouse** begins its nightly task of guiding ships to Honolulu. Built in 1899 on once remote terrain, the lighthouse was a difficult day's journey from Honolulu. A little more than a century later, it overlooks a coastal road, a ten-minute drive from downtown.

him to move, and Edgecombe relocated his family to a home in Honolulu. Then in 1942 Edgecombe was transferred to the mainland to take up a new post in Long Beach, California.

The shift to California finally brought to an end the wonder years of Carol Edgecombe Brown's childhood in Hawaii. To this day she remembers Diamond Head and her experiences here with great fondness. Although the tree that once held the family tree houses is long gone and the residence is, perhaps, a little less cozy, Brown is glad the old keeper's dwelling is still a home. "I think having Coast Guard personnel live here gives it all a real sense of permanence," she says.

It's early morning and Waikiki is not yet bustling. Soon, however, Honolulu's swank resort district will be teaming with tourists who have come here for a taste of paradise.

An Aloha Tower

Back during the days when Carol Edgecombe Brown lived with her family at the Diamond Head Lighthouse not far from Honolulu, Hawaii's capital city could claim another very different sort of lighthouse. Built down near the wharves in 1926, the 10-story Aloha Tower welcomed countless boatloads of tourists to Hawaii. For many years the tallest structure in Honolulu, the tower could be seen from miles at sea. No doubt arriving steamship passengers strained at the rails hoping to be the first to catch sight of it. For them the tower's fanciful art deco design must have seemed wondrously suggestive of the earthly paradise they were about enter.

Despite its appearance, however, the Aloha Tower had a serious, workaday purpose. It was built to function as a traffic control tower for Honolulu's bustling harbor, a job it still handles today. An amber light near the top of the tower signals inbound vessels when they may safely enter the harbor. Another light signals outbound ships when they have clearance to depart. Originally the tower functioned as a lighthouse as well. A powerful beacon was mounted just below the dome.

Although its beacon was removed many years ago, the tower remains the center of activity on the Honolulu waterfront. The hub of an upscale shopping and dining complex, the tower attracts droves of locals and tourists seeking a convenient place to relax, enjoy the scenery, and while away a few hours. Marking the hours is easy here since the tower sports four large clocks, one each facing north, south, east, and west. Some may find this an ironic touch, since Hawaii is known as a place where the passage of time is seldom noticed.

Like the Honolulu waterfront and its famous tower, Manny Silva embodies the timeless qualities of Hawaii. Now in his seventies, Silva lives in the city's lively Chinatown district, but he is frequently seen enjoying himself and singing traditional Hawaiian songs at the Aloha Tower Marketplace beside the harbor. As a child during the 1930s, Silva worked in this area, diving into the harbor's bright blue waters to snatch coins thrown by sailors and tourists.

"When I was a little guy, my dad was a hard-working man," says Silva. "But all his money went for food. So I made up my mind to find some way to earn a nickel so I could buy candy or go to the movies."

Silva joined the flocks of other Hawaiian children who dove for coins off the harbor piers and docks. Often the young divers gathered around the navy fighting ships that docked here to put sailors ashore for liberty. "We'd call the sailors Mac," says Silva. "We'd say, 'Hey Mac,

For most of human history, Hawaii remained hidden, less than 7,000 square miles of land lost in 60 million square miles of ocean. The Pacific provides Hawaii with stunning ocean vistas and also serves as a vital commercial link to the mainland. Lighthouses strengthen this lifeline by making navigation safer.

can you drop a coin in the water?' They would throw pennies, and we'd have three or four guys go into the water rushing for the pennies. We might get 12 or 15 cents for a whole day, and we would cherish that."

When grand passenger liners came into the harbor, the professional coin divers took over squeezing out children like Silva. "We were small guys, and they were big," Silva says. "If we went into the water while they were there, they would dip us under. They would sink us under the water because we were infringing on their trade."

When President Roosevelt sailed into the harbor on a navy cruiser in 1934, Silva and his companions were waiting by the water to dive for coins. Instead of diving, however, they

found themselves caught up in the spectacle. "We were ready to get in the water, but we wanted to see the president," says Silva. "He waved to us, and seeing such a great man was a very proud moment."

Seven years later, President Roosevelt made his historic "date that will live in infamy" speech after the Japanese bombed Pearl Harbor. These events and the great Pacific war that followed would forever change Honolulu and the islands as Silva and other Hawaiians had known them.

"That lady there, they camouflaged her," says Silva, indicating the old Aloha Tower. "They painted her all different colors."

Camouflage paint, blacked-out windows, and gun emplacements marred the Aloha Tower during the war. Afterwards the landmark returned to its former appearance, but by that time the waterfront district had lost much of its vitality and traditional Hawaiian character. The Honolulu airport replaced the harbor as Oahu's primary tourist portal, and the Hawaii of coin divers, hula, and the aloha song faded to little more than a memory.

Widening the Circle

D uring the early twentieth century, lighthouses proved their immense value to Hawaii by helping secure a reliable lifeline to the mainland. By the 1930s ships were bringing millions of tons of goods and materials and tens of thousands of tourists to this fabled island realm in the middle of the Pacific. Making sure the flood of passengers and cargo reached the islands safely required an even wider and more efficient circle of lights. An effort to extend the reach of Hawaii's guiding lights began

By the 1930s millions of tons of goods and materials and tens of thousands of tourists were making their way annually to this fabled paradise. Innovation was the key to sustaining the lights that guided ships here—lights needed to be more efficient if they were to cover more of the islands. A monument to that effort stands on the western approach to Honolulu Harbor—the **Barbers Point Lighthouse**.

about 1932, the same year Franklin Roosevelt was elected president. A monument to that effort stands at Barbers Point, marking the western approaches to Honolulu Harbor.

A smaller light tower had stood on Barbers Point since 1913, but its light was considered inadequate by mariners who depended on it to reach Honolulu. Even worse, the old light failed to provide sufficient early warning of the dangerous reef that lay just off shore. To correct these problems construction of a new light tower was begun in 1932.

The site was extremely difficult to reach. The construction crew arrived by way of a narrow gauge train ordinarily used to carry harvesters into the sugar cane fields. From the train the crew had to walk 2 miles over a rough wagon road. But by the spring of 1933, they had completed the 82-foot tower.

Originally the Barbers Point light tower was designed for an old-style lighting system. Plans called for it to be fitted with a Fresnel lens and a petroleum vapor lamp not unlike those in use before the introduction of electric bulbs in lighthouse lanterns. However, this plan was scrapped before the new light was placed in operation. What had started out as a classic lighthouse, very similar to those that had been built for 200 years, became an experiment in economy and technique.

"The 1930s was a period of transition," says Neil Gardis, an engineer who has helped restore several Hawaiian lighthouses, including the one at Barbers Point. "This particular lighthouse was built in the midst of that transition."

Unlike more traditional lighthouses with their glassed-in lantern rooms, the tower at **Barbers Point** supports an exposed airport-style beacon. Impervious to wind and rain, the Barbers Point beacon requires little maintenance and no full-time keeper.

Instead of a heavy Fresnel lens, the tower received a relatively light and inexpensive rotating electric beacon much like those used at airports. Traditional lighthouses had a lantern room enclosed all around by windows to protect their fragile lenses from the wind and rain, but at Barbers Point none of this was needed.

"Rotating beacons are weatherproof," Gardis says. "And in some instances their light shines farther than that of a lamp and Fresnel lens."

This new lighting system was to have a profound effect on the old-time profession of

Neil Gardis

lighthouse keeper. "The whole business of operating a lighthouse was reduced to the replacement of a bulb from time to time," says Gardis. "Lighthouse keeping became an antique almost overnight."

Special Beacons for Hawaii

Hawaii confronted mariners with nearly 1,000 miles of craggy coastline. Many of the most dangerous areas, where navigational lights were most needed, were far too rugged and remote for ordinary light stations. To mark them and guide mariners through Hawaii's unforgiving waters, lighthouse engineers were forced to adopt fresh technologies. Automation was critical to lighting the islands.

Some island lights are milestones to lighthouse innovation. Stalwart concrete and stainless steel structures, they were designed to withstand Hawaii's open-ocean climate and unstable terrain. Requiring no on-site keepers, they stand their vigils alone.

Some such navigational aides are called "Vega lights." Made in New Zealand, Vega lights are relatively modest and inexpensive rotating beacons operated by timers or small computers. Their power is drawn from batteries recharged by solar panels. Continuously monitored by way of radio signals from distant Coast Guard stations, Vegas may guide mariners for months or even years at a time without human assistance. However, when maintenance is needed, reaching these isolated "robot" lights can be quite difficult.

The Coast Guard units assigned to maintain these lights undertake their often dangerous tasks with military efficiency. Their work may carry them across many miles of ocean to remote scraps of rock that can be reached only by air.

"We are responsible for all the lighthouses and shore aids in the Hawaiian Islands," says Chief Mike Martin, a member of the Coast Guard's Aides to Navigation Team Hawaii. "We've got ten major aides—lighthouses—and almost a hundred minor lights on nine different islands."

One of the team's minor lights is located atop Lehua Rock on the western side of the extensive Hawaiian chain. Perched more than 700 feet above the Pacific on the rim of an ancient volcano, it is a typical Vega light, completely automated and far smaller than a traditional lighthouse. Considered "minor" only because of its size, this navigational aid is vital to mariners who count on its beacon to warn them away from Lehua Rock and other deadly obstacles. Usually quite dependable, the Lehua Rock beacon goes dark occasionally, and when it does the Aides to Navigation Team Hawaii must act quickly.

The crater rim—a knife blade of reddish-brown stone—can only be approached from above. To reach the light and make repairs, a helicopter is indispensable. In most such situations, the team can count on a lift from the local Coast Guard air station. "Often the only way to get there is by helicopter," says Martin. "Without the air station we couldn't do our job."

After a helicopter flight of more than an hour, the team arrived at Lehua Rock. Then, maneuvering with great care, the pilot lowered two members of the team down onto the crater rim in a basket. There they set to work on the malfunctioning Vega. Realizing their helicopter might be forced to abandon them at any moment, the repair crew made every second count. Ailing navigational lights are not the top priority for Coast Guard pilots who must remain constantly available in case their aircraft is needed for search-and-rescue operations. Should their pilot be called on to assist some foundering ship or drowning seaman, the crew might very well be stranded until he returns—hours or even days later.

A Coast Guard helicopter lowers the basket to Lehua Rock.

Two Coast Guardsmen approach the light tower at Lehua Rock.

Aides to Navigation team members and their pilots must share the inconveniences and dangers of such missions. Storms are always a threat, and the updrafts and crosswinds created by the mountainous islands can be hard to negotiate. Bird strikes are a particular concern. The islands harbor a sizable avian population, and an errant flock may appear seemingly out of nowhere. If a helicopter or airplane hits a large bird, engines or instruments may be damaged, with disastrous results.

However, this particular mission to Lehua Rock went off without a hitch. Having made their repairs, the team was hoisted back aboard the helicopter for the return flight to the air station on Oahu. That same evening the automated navigational aid on Lehua Rock was once more lighting the way for mariners.

Chief Mike Martin and others like him are the lighthouse keepers of today. Unlike their predecessors, they seldom climb the spiraling iron steps inside a light tower, and rarely live near the lights they keep. But they are nonetheless dedicated.

"Mariners and even airplane pilots really depend on the lights to give them a sense of confidence," says Chief Martin. "So we're going to go out there and make sure the lights are working properly. That's our job."

Hawaii's First Lighthouse Marked a Royal Capital

N ot all of Hawaii's lighthouses were built in places as remote as the Lehua Rock crater rim. In fact, Hawaii's first true lighthouse stood at the very heart of the islands in the royal city of Lahaina located on the western side of Maui. The Hawaiian ruler Kamehameha I established his capital at Lahaina after he unified the islands through conquest during the 1790s. Foreign diplomats, merchants, and missionaries flocked there to visit Kamehameha and his descendants. After 1840 their vessels were guided into harbor by a lighthouse, among the first in all of what is now the western United States.

Although it served mariners for more than seventy-five years, nothing is left of that early lighthouse. The sentinel that replaced it in 1916, however, still guides ships, and its relatively simple, pyramidal tower remains in excellent condition.

"It's in top shape," says Keoki Freeland, director of the Lahaina Restoration Society. Born and raised in Lahaina, Freeland is quite proud of the old lighthouse, which has been a familiar sight to him since he was a boy. "Except for painting, very little work has ever been done to it."

The existing Lahaina Lighthouse has thick masonry walls that taper inward. A small platform at the top holds the lighting mechanism, while an exterior ladder provides access for maintenance. Except for a small control panel and the cables that supply power for the light, the interior walls are bare.

"You see a lot of this type of lighthouse around Hawaii," Freeland says. "It's a very simple, rugged, and durable design. The wide base keeps the tower safe from strong winds."

Like most Hawaiian communities, Lahaina is subject to powerful gales, which may blow in off the Pacific without warning. But over the years the city, its lighthouses, and people have faced many other stresses as well. The storm winds of political and cultural change have raked Lahaina for more than two centuries.

Beginning in the late eighteenth century, clipper ships and other merchant vessels regularly crossed the 7,000-mile-wide Pacific to load rich cargoes in China. Many of those ships stopped off in Hawaii to take on food and fresh water or repair masts and sails damaged by sharp Pacific gales. Lahaina was a favorite port of call.

During the early nineteenth century, whalers came to Lahaina from New England. "They whaled up in Alaska and then came back to Hawaii during the winter months," says Freeland. "As many as 500 whaling ships would be anchored off Lahaina during the winter."

A key historical attraction at Lahaina is the museum ship *Carthaginian*, a replica of the supply schooners that made annual trips to Hawaii during the whaling boom. Vessels like the *Carthaginian* were not whalers themselves. Rather they brought loads of rope, nails, tools, canvas, and other supplies needed by the whaling ships, which were likely to work the Pacific for up to four years before returning home to New England.

Often cooped up aboard their ships for months at a time, homesick whaling crews turned Lahaina into something of a Wild West frontier town. "You can just imagine what it was like," says Freeland. "There was a huge conflict between the whalers and the missionaries who had come here at about the same time."

After the capital shifted to Honolulu in 1845 and whaling fell into decline, Lahaina quieted down. But many years later, during World War II, Lahaina was once again invaded by sailors on liberty. "There were 102 ships of the Pacific fleet anchored out here when I was just a little boy," Freeland says. "Seamen came ashore in waves of 10,000, and they turned the streets white with uniforms."

Keoki Freeland points out the limited space in the Lahaina tower.

Now, more than half a century later, the fighting ships have been replaced by luxury cruise liners. With its royal roots, quaint streets, and historic buildings, Lahaina has become an important Hawaiian tourist attraction. Ironically, most who come here take little notice of the old lighthouse, which along with its predecessor, made possible so much of Lahaina's rich and tumultuous history.

A good way to see the Lahaina Light is from the deck of one of the ferries that frequent the harbor. Some Lahaina ferries offer a short cruise across the Auau Channel to the delightful and bucolic island of Lanai, where another very different window remains open on Hawaii's past. At one time the Dole Company owned the entire island, using it for what was literally the world's largest pineapple plantation. Lanai remains quite rural and, like so much

Thousands of visitors arrive by cruise ship to the port of Lahaina, home to one of Hawaii's most accessible and historic lighthouses. The first lighthouse in the Hawaiian Islands marked Lahaina, King Kamehameha's royal capital on Maui. Built in 1840, it was torn down in 1916 and replaced by the slender pyramidal tower at seen at left.

Among the many historic attractions of Lahaina is the sailing ship *Carthaginian*, replica of a supply schooner that served the Pacific whaling fleet during the nineteenth century. Berthed near the **Lahaina tower,** it serves as a museum.

of Hawaii, extremely beautiful, but Dole and most of the pineapples are gone. Today the island is owned by the Castle & Cooke Corporation, which opened two luxury resorts here during the 1990s. Visitors with a penchant to explore the island will find much to interest them, including unspoiled beaches, dramatic cliffs, and ancient ruins. As a bonus, on their trips across the channel to and from Lanai, they will be guided by Hawaii's oldest navigational beacon, the Lahaina Lighthouse.

Fiery Pele Spares a Lighthouse

To the south of Maui across a broad ocean channel more than 30 miles wide is the giant island that gave our nation's fiftieth state its name. Known locally as the "Big Island," Hawaii is a wild and varied land with Scottish-like highlands in the north, sloping coasts to the east and west, and a virtual moonscape to the south. Encompassing more than 4,000 square miles, the Big Island is larger than all the other islands combined—and it keeps getting bigger.

Ten thousand feet above sea level fumes mighty Kilauea, among the latest in a 3,000-mile-long string of volcanoes that have erupted one after the other over many millions of years. Here on the Big Island, Hawaii's volcanoes are still raising new land from the sea. Thanks to the almost constant eruptions of Kilauea, the island is still growing, currently at a rate of about five acres per year. According to Hawaiian legend, all this is the handiwork of Pele, the fire goddess. For those who build and maintain lighthouses, Pele's fiery acts of creation pose unique challenges. Light stations on the Big Island may be threatened, not only by storm winds, high water, and corrosion, but also by unstoppable rivers of lava.

Built in 1934, the Cape Kumukahi Lighthouse marks the easternmost point in the Hawaiian chain.

Sizzling lava tumbles into the Pacific off Cape Kumukahi.

Lava flows from Hawaii's active Kilauea Volcano.

When the tower rose on Cape Kumukahi in 1934, it's mission was to mark Hawaii's most eastern point and greet ships approaching the islands from the Panama Canal. The 125-foot skeletal steel tower was a new approach for lighthouses. Quick to construct, it was also more forgiving of shifting ground. The light tower at Cape Kumukahi was miraculously spared by a 1960 lava flow.

Perhaps most strategic of all the island lights, its beacon is the first to greet ships approaching Hawaii from the Panama Canal. To handle this important mission, engineers selected an open-sided steel skeleton design for the station's 125-foot tower. Relatively inexpensive and easy to erect, the skeleton tower was considered especially appropriate for the unstable Kumukahi site with its constantly shifting volcanic rock. What is more, the tower's exposed girders would allow high winds to pass right through its walls with little or no effect. For more than twenty-five years this durable structure and its beacon served mariners without incident. But Pele had a surprise in store for the Kumukahi Lighthouse and its keepers.

In January of 1960 an ominous crack appeared behind the village of Kapoho, not far from the lighthouse. Soon fountains of magma were spurting high into the air and forming a lake of red-hot lava. Inexorably the lava flooded toward the ocean, burying Kapoho along with several square miles of rich farmland. The Kumukahi peninsula and its lighthouse lay directly in the path of the flood.

Another advantage of a steel-skeleton tower is that it can be torn down, moved, and reassembled on another site, but there was no time to do that in this case. Descending on Kumukahi before government officials or the Coast Guard could respond, the relentless lava obliterated the station keepers' cottages and storage buildings. By the time the lava reached the Pacific, it had destroyed every man-made object on the peninsula—except for one. Inexplicably, the lava wall had parted near the base of the steel tower and spared the Kumukahi Light.

Kimo Awai

Some see a deeper meaning in this story. They believe there may be reason Pele spared the lighthouse. Kimo Awai, a teacher of ancient Hawaiian rituals, believes the tower stands on a sacred site. "The Hawaiian word for this place is Vahipana," Awai says. "Vahipana means sacred place."

According to Awai, Hawaiians believe that all the earth is sacred. This far eastern point of the Big Island is especially so because it is here that the first light of the morning sun can be seen. And even a modern, man-made contraption, such as a steel light tower, can serve a sacred purpose. "Maybe the lighthouse was spared because the elements knew it preserved the sanctity of man," Kimo Awai says. "As long as the light shines, people are safe."

Kings and Sugar Cane

Some 90 miles north of the Kumukahi peninsula, on the far side of the Big Island, the rugged lava gives way to the rich soil and green valleys of the Kohala region. Here was the birthplace of Kamehameha I, Hawaii's greatest king. It was from Kohala that Kamehameha launched his drive to conquer and unify the islands.

For many years Hawaii was ruled by another king—the sugar industry—and it, too, had roots in Kohala. Huge quantities of sugar cane began to be planted about the middle of the nineteenth century. Vast fields of this big-money crop once blanketed the fertile Kohala region and similar lowland districts throughout the islands. Most of the sugar mills are closed now, but a key relic from the days of King Sugar remains.

The Kohala Point Lighthouse was built in 1932, not long before the Hawaiian sugar industry began its long, slow decline. The light marks a natural landing, which may have been used for maritime purposes for as long as fifteen hundred years. During the era of the sugar plantations, the light guided freighters to their anchorage off Kohala Point, where they waited to fill their holds with heavy bags of Hawaii's "white gold."

Subject to high winds and fierce rains, the anchorage was not nearly as well protected as some in Hawaii. The lighthouse was exposed to these same conditions and had to contend with earthquakes as well. Even so, with a foundation of reinforced concrete and a superstructure of welded steel, the tower has stood up to all the punishment the Pacific could throw at it.

"This was our connection to the world," Mike Gomes says of the landing and its lighthouse. A land manager and amateur historian, Gomes is descended from four generations of sugar workers, and he knows what life was like here when the tower was built almost seventy years ago. "Roads were nonexistent, so boat landings of this nature were key."

The landing made it possible for the plantations to bring in supplies and equipment and ship their product to market, but the sugar workers and their families also found important uses for Kohala Point. "The lighthouse was a place for plantation workers to get away from the workaday world," Gomes says. "They held horse races here, played baseball, and went fishing."

To this day the area around the lighthouse remains a popular playground, one that is not found in tourist guidebooks but is well known to locals. Families enjoy barbecues and picnics within site of the lighthouse. There is plenty of hiking and fishing available, and young people ride dirt bikes over the well-worn paths. Like the sugar workers of a century ago, members of the Kohala community still consider this a place of refuge.

A traditional refuge of a much more serious sort can be found on the far western shores of the Big Island at a place called Honaunau. During the sixteenth century, Honaunau became a haven for violators of the strict *kapu* system that governed social behavior. The kapu code made it illegal to step on a chief's shadow, for a commoner to touch a member of the upper class, for men and women to eat together, or for women to eat bananas. These and many similar acts were considered taboo, and anyone committing them was likely to be put to death. Execution might be avoided, however, if the kapu violator could somehow reach the temple

Another of Hawaii's automated navigational beacons, the **Kohala Point Lighthouse** on the north shore of the Big Island has guided mariners since 1932. Kohala Point was the last of the classic towers built in the days of King Sugar. It marks a natural landing used by mariners for about fifteen centuries.

In 1779 a procession of Hawaiian canoes returned the body of Captain James Cook to British ships anchored in Kealakekua Bay. The famed explorer had been struck down on shore during a confrontation over a stolen boat.

complex at Honaunau or some other such sanctuary.

Honaunau lost much of its importance after the kapu system was abandoned in 1819. The Puuhonua O Honaunau National Historical Park now celebrates the sanctuary's intriguing past. Its great stone wall, restored temple, and carved images make it a must-see for anyone interested in Hawaii as it was before the arrival of Europeans.

Coincidentally, only a few miles to the north is Kealakekua Bay, where Captain James Cook first made contact with Hawaiians in 1778. The bay proved no safe haven for Cook, who was killed there in 1779. However, sea turtles, spinner dolphins, other visitors from the open Pacific may have better luck here than did the famous British explorer. Kealakekua is now a major marine preserve. For human visitors the bay offers some of Hawaii's best snorkeling, diving, and kayaking.

A GLANCE AT HAWAII'S
HUMAN HISTORY

Much of Hawaii's approximately seventeen hundred years of history is shrouded in legend. It can be traced back to at least 300 A.D., by which time the first Polynesian settlers had landed on the islands. Likely they came from the Marquesas Islands in the South Pacific, daring the 3,000-mile crossing in twin-hulled voyaging canoes. Skilled farmers and craftsmen, they tilled the land and made efficient use of the islands' natural resources. For most islanders, life revolved around their ohana or extended family, which might number several hundred members.

During the twelfth and thirteenth centuries, fresh waves of Polynesians from Tahiti and Samoa invaded the islands, sweeping away much of the thousand-year-old Hawaiian culture. Establishing a more rigid social order with themselves at the top, the newcomers introduced the concept of kapu or taboo. Under the kapu system a wide variety of activities were strictly forbidden. The punishment for violations was usually death.

The Spanish were likely the first European voyagers to stumble onto the islands, but it was the British who would first announce their existence to the world. The explorer Captain James Cook sailed into Hawaiian waters in 1778 and anchored his ships Discovery and Resolution in the Big Island's Kealakekua Bay. Cook was at first honored as a god by the native Hawaiians, but they soon realized he was not divine. The year after his arrival, Cook was killed in a confrontation with locals over a stolen boat. Cook was followed by other explorers, and during the final decades of the eighteenth century, merchant seamen began to use the islands as a convenient stopover on their lengthy voyages across the Pacific.

Queen Liliuokalani, the last reigning monarch in Hawaii

In 1791 an ambitious Kohala chief named Kamehameha launched a successful campaign to unify the islands under a single monarch. Using cannon and other weapons he had obtained from Westerners, Kamehameha blasted his way onto one island after another. With the conquest of Oahu in 1795, the unification of Hawaii was all but complete. Kauai in the far north held out for several more years, but in 1809 its chief finally ceded the island.

Kamehameha died in 1819 and was followed by rulers who lacked his political acumen or skill as a warrior. They gradually lost control of the islands to Westerners, especially American businessmen, who increasingly treated Hawaii as one large sugar plantation. To work the cane fields and operate the sugar mills, laborers were imported from all over the Pacific, and eventually native Hawaiians became a minority in their own country. In an attempt to modernize Hawaii, its monarchs abandoned the old kapu system, embraced Christianity, and adopted Western styles, but they could not stem the rising tide of foreign power. Hawaii's last ruler, Queen Liliuokalani, was overthrown by a so-called "committee" of American businessmen in 1893.

In 1898 the islands were absorbed by the United States, and they became an official U.S. territory two years later. The bombing of Pearl Harbor in 1941 and the great Pacific war that followed emphasized the strategic importance of the islands. In 1959 a star was added to the U.S. flag to represent our nation's fiftieth state—Hawaii.

Haunting Beauty and a Haunted Past

Positioned near the middle of the Hawaiian chain, the long and narrow island of Molokai is home to a historical park even more haunting than the one at Honaunau. During the late 1800s, Hansen's disease ran rampant through Hawaii. Dreaded throughout the world, the disfiguring disease, more widely known as leprosy, was considered so contagious that its victims were forcibly segregated from other islanders. Most were shipped to an isolation settlement on Molokai's rugged Kalaupapa peninsula. Today the settlement is part of Kalaupapa National Historical Park, which marks this grim chapter in the Hawaiian saga.

Kalaupapa's tragic past contrasts sharply with the stark natural beauty of Molokai. By almost any measure, this lightly populated island must be considered one of the most remarkable places on the planet. Like Hawaii's other islands, it was formed by repeated volcanic eruptions. On Molokai these fiery convulsions left behind bright orange soils, yellow beaches, and mile-high peaks deeply crevassed by erosion. Perhaps most impressive of the island's astounding geological features are the verdant northern cliffs that drop some 2,000 feet straight down into the Pacific. Forming an almost impenetrable wall more than 40 miles long, these ramparts are both an amazement to visitors and a deadly threat to shipping.

To help mariners keep their distance from the ship-killing cliffs, a lighthouse was built on Kalaupapa Point in 1908. Getting materials and construction crews to the faraway, essentially roadless site made this an unusually expensive lighthouse. The entire station, including the tower, keeper's residence, and storage buildings cost the U.S. government $60,000—a substantial sum at that time.

The station quickly proved its worth to mariners, however. The tower's 4-foot-thick, octagonal walls soared to a height of 138 feet, making this the tallest lighthouse on the Pacific. A concrete staircase gave the tower added strength, while providing access to the lantern room at the top. Its revolving light,

The cliffs of Molokai's northern coast are more than 40 miles long east to west and reach up to 2,000 feet in height. This daunting and impressive feature made the peninsula of this island all but inaccessible during the nineteenth and early twentieth centuries. Even today, wise mariners keep their distance from this rugged coast.

once rated at two million candlepower, shined out to sea from an elevation of more than 200 feet and could reach ships up to 25 miles away, giving them ample time to change course and avoid the menacing rocks at the foot of the Molokai cliffs.

The station's rotating lens was driven by a clockwork mechanism powered by a set of weights slowly descending through the center of the tower. Every few hours the device had to be "rewound" by raising the weights. This repetitive task and many other such chores made Kalaupapa a labor-intensive light station. Until it was fully automated in 1972, the lighthouse required constant attention by its keepers and their assistants.

In 1940 six-year-old Fred Robins Jr. arrived at Kalaupapa with his father who had recently been appointed keeper. As it did for nearly everyone who came to live in this extra-ordinary place, Kalaupapa was to leave its mark on him. His years at the light station now stand out among his most powerful memories.

"I have a lot of history back there," says Robins. "And it will stay with me for the rest of my life."

In most ways Robins belonged to a typical lighthouse family. His grandfather and great-grandfather had also been lighthouse keepers. He himself was born and spent his earliest years at the Kilauea Point Lighthouse on Kauai, where his father worked before coming to Molokai.

At the Kalaupapa light, young Robins pitched in to help with lighthouse chores. "I did a lot of things there to help my dad as I was growing up," Robins says. "I would sweep and mop inside the tower, help with the painting and polishing, and crank the counterweight to get the lens spinning."

To raise the weights, Robins had to climb the spiraling staircase inside the tower. There were 198 steps in all. "It was quite a ways to go," says Robins, who mounted the Kalaupapa tower steps thousands of times.

Fred Robins Jr.

Stair climbing was a chore common to nearly every light station, but the lantern room at the top of the stairs provided an experience that was anything but ordinary. Its windows offered a view, not just of the vast Pacific or the daunting Molokai cliffs, but also of the Kalaupapa isolation settlement not far from the lighthouse compound. Over time the settlement, with its strictly quarantined community of disease victims, was to make a deep impression on the young lighthouse keeper's son.

Until new drugs developed during the 1950s made it possible to cure leprosy, those who contracted the disease lived under a virtual death sentence. For them Kalaupapa was a place of loneliness and despair. Forcibly separated from homes and families, they lived in what was essentially a prison made escape proof by rough seas and unscalable cliffs.

In 1908 construction began on the **Kalaupapa Point Lighthouse**, on the lone peninsula along the coast. When completed, Kalaupapa became the tallest lighthouse in the Pacific, standing over 138 feet tall. The tower's strength is in its octagonal walls, which are four-feet thick, and a cement staircase that bolsters the entire tower and leads to the light above.

Kalaupapa lighthouse keepers and their families rarely mingled with patients at the isolation settlement. Contacts were discouraged by both wire fences and custom. In time, however, Robins would breach these barriers and reach out to his neighbors. "My parents were very protective," says Robins. "But as I grew older I got to love everybody. As far as I was concerned, we were all one family."

For many Kalaupapa patients, the lighthouse beacon was an emotional anchor, a warm reminder of the wider world from which they had been excluded. Occasionally patients were invited to the lighthouse to see the mechanism that produced its powerful flash.

"When they weren't under the eye of the administration, you know, they were invited to come up to the lighthouse," says Robins. "I'd say, come on up and take a look inside. And they would come in, go up to the light, and see how beautiful it looked during the night."

By 1959 patients were allowed to wander, not just to the lighthouse, but wherever they wished. New medicines had set them free from their disease, if not of the scars it had left. Many returned to the lives they had left behind when they first came to Kalaupapa, but a handful of former patients chose to remain and live out their lives in what was now their home.

In 1980 the settlement came under the protection of the National Park Service. Known today as the Kalaupapa National Historical Park, it attracts a small but steady stream of tourists keenly interested in the poignant human dramas that unfolded there. Visitors must be quite determined, as no one comes to Kalaupapa by accident. The only access is by air or by means of a narrow winding trail descending the precipitous cliffs above the peninsula. Some chose to hike the 2-mile access trail and negotiate its twenty-six switchbacks on foot, but most visitors wisely elect to ride down on the backs of surefooted mules. Views along the way are, to say the least, spectacular.

For Fred Robins Jr. Kalaupapa is not a historical monument, but rather his beloved childhood home. It fills him with memories of growing up there and of people, some still living, others long ago passed away. "The light itself gives me a tremendous feeling," he says.

Robins is proud of his experience here. "I let people know where I was raised and they look at me. 'Kalaupapa?' And I say, 'Yes, Kalaupapa. That's where I was raised.'"

The Garden Isle

Like Molokai, the island of Kauai is a place of great beauty. Both the farthest north and oldest of the major islands, Kauai was born in Hawaii's volcanic fires more than six million years ago. Time and weather have tuned it into a wonderland where pleated cliffs tower over azure waves and white sand beaches, cold streams race through yawning chasms, and rare birds sing in the canopies of dense hillside rain forests. The island's rich topsoils generate such a lush blanket of emerald green vegetation that Hawaiians have nicknamed Kauai their "Garden Isle."

Kauai's spectacular scenery makes it one of Hawaii's most popular destinations. In fact the tourists who come here each year—mostly by air from Honolulu—far outnumber the island's largely rural population. Visitors are rarely if ever disappointed by what they discover on Kauai. In addition to its natural marvels, the island offers golf, swimming, snorkeling, surfing, hiking, horseback riding, and much more.

Palms frame the 80-foot tower of the **Nawiliwili Lighthouse** on verdant Kauai. Equipped with a modern, weather-resistant beacon, the tower needs no lantern room.

Many visitors take time out from all those activities for a walk through the Kilauea Point National Wildlife Refuge on the north side of the island. This relatively small, clifftop refuge serves as a sanctuary for frigate birds, Laysan albatrosses, red-footed boobies, wedge-tailed shearwaters, and a variety of other Pacific seabirds.

"This is primarily a seabird nesting habitat," says wildlife biologist Kathleen Viernes. She believes the birds flock to Kilauea Point because it is so prominent and easy to locate. "Birds looking for new places to nest hit this beacon of land sticking out into the ocean."

Waterfalls on the island of Kauai

Wildlife biologist Kathleen Viernes

Interestingly, Kilauea Point refuge is the site of another sort of beacon, a veteran lighthouse. Built in 1913, the Kilauea Point Lighthouse is no longer in active service, but it guided several generations of mariners. Poised near the top of a cliff overlooking the Pacific, it marked the far northwestern edge of the primary Hawaiian chain. Its light was focused by a giant, second-order Fresnel lens shaped like a clamshell. Shining out over the ocean from an elevation of more than 200 feet, the light could be seen from ships more than 20 miles away. Passenger liners, freighters, and naval vessels approaching the islands from the northwest and the Orient relied on the Kilauea Point Light to guide them in from the open Pacific. Nowadays that same service is provided by a small, automated beacon located not far from the original tower.

Although no longer in use as an aide to navigators, the beautiful clamshell lens remains in place at the top of the 53-foot tower. "The lens is clearly a jewel," says refuge site manager Dave Aplin. "That's what gave the Kilauea light its distinctive double flash every ten seconds. You can see the flash panels—the bull's-eyes or owl's-eyes—that magnified and concentrated the light."

When the beacon was automated in 1976, the Coast Guard gave the tower, lens, and keeper's dwelling to the National Fish and Wildlife Service. The gift proved to have been a

Built in 1913, **Kilauea Point Lighthouse** was once the northernmost beacon in the Hawaiian chain. The lighthouse itself is only 59 feet tall but sits on a towering cliff that puts its focal plane some 217 feet above the water, allowing it to be seen some 20 miles out to sea. No longer active, Kilauea Point serves as a picturesque centerpiece for a popular wildlife refuge. Visitors enjoy close-up views of nesting seabirds as well as the historic lighthouse.

Nowadays, Kilauea Point is a beacon for Pacific seabirds such as this albatross pair.

worthy one, for today the fine old lighthouse with its gleaming lens is the centerpiece, the "jewel" of the 200-acre wildlife sanctuary.

"The lighthouse is a magnet," Aplin says. "It brings people here who may never have visited a national wildlife refuge. But when they get here, they see the spinner dolphins and humpback whales in the sea. They see the albatrosses and the boobies flying over, and they really appreciate the natural community we have here."

When they leave, refuge visitors often take with them an enhanced appreciation of our natural environment and of the demands nature makes on all species—even our own—in their struggle to survive. "Many people come here just to see the lighthouse," says Viernes. "Then they see the birds flying all around them. They see the birds very close up, and they leave educated about wildlife."

Some of the birds that frequent the point are quite large and impressive. The frigate bird, for instance, has a wingspan of 7 feet or more and can fly great distances over the ocean. Albatrosses have an even longer wingspan and have been sighted soaring over the ocean hundreds of miles from the nearest land.

For Aplin, who knows the history of this area well, these huge birds may occasionally call to mind that even larger bird, the "Bird of Paradise" that soared over the Pacific on the morning of June 29, 1927. Aviators Lester Maitland and Albert Hegenberger, whose story was told at the beginning of this chapter, might have missed the islands altogether, but for the Kilauea Point Lighthouse.

Although its big clamshell lens is lit up now only on special occasions, the Kilauea Point Light Station remains a key Hawaiian sentinel and guidepost. While the old light tower serves as a reminder of Hawaii's extraordinarily rich natural and human heritage, the modern aerobeacon located nearby continues to guide mariners. This light, like the others that ring the archipelago, still calls travelers to the islands.

"That is important," says Aplin. "That is an important story because we're still out in the middle of the ocean. Look at a satellite photograph of the Pacific and you'll see these tiny dots. You will find nowhere else on earth where there's a bigger mote around a group of islands."

The mission of guiding explorers, mariners, settlers, traders, and tourists is shared by all of Hawaii's lights. Whatever their size, shape, or type of beacon, they brighten the shores of an island chain that would otherwise be lost in the dark vastness of the Pacific. These lights not only mark a coast but connect people one to another over otherwise impossible distances.

Shaped something like a clamshell, this huge Fresnel lens once focused the **Kilauea Point** light signal.

ALASKA

*Lights of
the Last Frontier*

Alaska is a remarkably isolated, far-flung area, with the lowest population density of any U.S. state. And yet nearly everything about Alaska, called the Great Land, seems larger than life. It is the largest state in the United States; its Mount McKinley is the highest point in North America; its Wrangell–St. Elias National Park is one of the largest in the world; and it has the longest coastline in the country. Alaska's coastline, in particular, is key to Alaskan transportation and commerce. The lighthouses here help to keep its waterways humming.

Lighthouses of the Great Land

Located on the seaward tip of uninhabited Kayak Island about 300 miles southeast of Anchorage, the Cape St. Elias Lighthouse is in many ways the epitome of an Alaskan light station. As with the state's other lighthouses, it cannot be reached by road. The nearest town is the thriving fishing community of Cordova, about a hour away by bush plane. Partly because it is so remote, the Coast Guard has automated the Cape St. Elias

Cape St. Elias Lighthouse

beacon and more or less abandoned the station's structures. But like several other historic Alaskan lighthouses, this one has acquired some diligent friends.

Several years ago John and Toni Bocci came to Kayak Island to enjoy a summer camping trip. "We got dropped off on the east side of the island, did some beachcombing, and camped out for four days," says Toni Bocci. "When the pilot picked us up, he flew us back down around the cape. That was the first time I had ever seen it."

As the plane swept past the cape, it rounded a 500-foot-tall, sail-shaped rock rising like a giant rhinoceros horn from the end of a mile-long beach. Beyond the rock, clustered among the boulders at the opposite end of the beach, was a collection of weathered buildings, the remains

The **Cape St. Elias Lighthouse** isn't the most obvious landmark on remote Kayak Island. The stunning Pinnacle Rock, at the cape's seaward end, rises 500 feet above the Pacific.

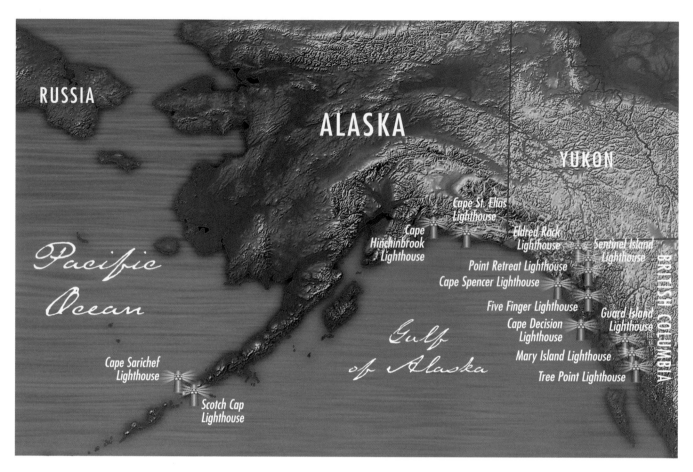

RUSSIA

ALASKA

YUKON

Pacific Ocean

Cape St. Elias Lighthouse

Cape Hinchinbrook Lighthouse

Eldred Rock Lighthouse

Sentinel Island Lighthouse

Point Retreat Lighthouse

Cape Spencer Lighthouse

Five Finger Lighthouse

Cape Decision Lighthouse

Guard Island Lighthouse

BRITISH COLUMBIA

Gulf of Alaska

Mary Island Lighthouse

Tree Point Lighthouse

Cape Sarichef Lighthouse

Scotch Cap Lighthouse

of the Cape St. Elias Lighthouse. "That's really a cool place," Toni told her husband John. "I want to go there someday."

A year or so after their camping trip, the Boccis noticed a newspaper advertisement that included the Cape St. Elias Lighthouse among a number of U.S. Coast Guard light stations available for lease to either nonprofit groups or individuals.

The Boccis inquired about a lease. Applications were supposed to be competitive, but the Boccis got their lease with little trouble. As it turned out, they were the only ones who applied for Cape St. Elias. And so was born the Cape St. Elias Lightkeepers Association— its purpose to preserve this historic landmark and make it accessible to the public. The Boccis know their job will be a big one.

Cape St. Elias has long been considered among the least accessible places along the entire coast of North America. Wise mariners keep their distance from the cape, for these waters are fraught with danger. Swirling currents combine with an omnipresent blanket of fog to make precise navigation all but impossible, while rocks and shoals lurk just beneath the surface waiting to tear open the hulls of any vessel that strays off course. For many years the government did little or nothing to help mariners avoid these hazards. Then in 1912 the lighthouse tender *Armeria* wrecked while placing a buoy here. This incident proved so embarrassing for maritime officials that Congress soon appropriated funds for a permanent light station.

The **Cape St. Elias Lighthouse** seems lost in the magnificence of its surroundings. Established in 1916, the station had full-time keepers until 1974. Cut off from the outside world for months at a time, station crews had to endure long stretches of complete isolation. The Cape St. Elias Lighthouse Association is working to preserve the historic landmark and make it accessible to the public.

"As near as we can tell from the journals, the construction of the entire reservation took two years and three months," says John Bocci. "The light was first lit on September 16, 1916, and we have to assume that most of the buildings were finished well before that time."

The original Cape St. Elias beacon was focused by a third-order Fresnel lens, and though powerful, it was never particularly effective. The 85-foot elevation of the lantern room limited the range of the light, which in any case was nearly always obscured by fog. Even so, an inadequate light was considered far better than nothing by the mariners forced to rely on its warning to steer them safely past the cape.

The tender *Armeria* signals trouble by displaying an inverted flag on her stern. The *Armeria* wrecked off Cape St. Elias in 1912 while servicing a nearby buoy. Soon afterward, a permanent light station was established here to prevent other such accidents.

To keep the light in operation, station personnel remained on duty constantly, in stints of a year or more at a time. Theirs was a lonely existence, broken only rarely by the infrequent visits of supply ships or the delivery of a piece or two of mail dropped off by some passing vessel. More than a few keepers considered this the "worst lighthouse duty station in America." No doubt the station's Coast Guard crewmen were happy enough to leave when the light was automated and the buildings boarded up in 1974.

Weather and time have been hard on the station's structures, especially during the decades since the station was automated. "The reservation consists of the tower itself, a four-bedroom, two-story keeper's house, a winch house, a boathouse, and a shop," says John Bocci. "All are in various stages of disrepair."

John Bocci examines earthquake damage.

Of particular concern is the deteriorated condition of the bricks and mortar that were used during construction of the station more than eighty-five years ago. In all, laborers made some 63,000 bricks using sand gathered from the adjacent beach. The bricks contain a high concentration of salt, which has caused them to crumble over time.

Far more destructive than salt, however, was the massive earthquake that rolled across coastal Alaska in 1964. "The earthquake raised the land around here by approximately 7 feet," says John Bocci. "You can see where it cracked the brickwork on some of the buildings. There are fractures in the light tower and the main house. The earthquake damage has contributed to the general deterioration."

The Boccis and their association hope to reverse the station's decline. "Without maintenance these buildings are going to be history soon," John Bocci says. "Our main objective is to get a roof on the buildings and get some drainage around them to dry out the foundations. At that point we can start to consider what it's going to take to make it pretty."

Volunteers deliver supplies to the Cape St. Elias Lighthouse.

From the point of view of Toni Bocci, Cape St. Elias and its lighthouse could hardly be made more attractive. She finds the station's setting even more engaging than its historic structures; she is fascinated by Pinnacle Rock and the changing moods of the weather systems that gather around it. "It holds the weather and has its own weather patterns," she says. "And it houses an array of wildlife. At the bottom there's a sea lion rookery, and there are birds of all sorts. It's a never-ending, always-changing show."

In the late afternoons, as sunset approaches, the Boccis like to relax and enjoy the show—"the horizon and the changing clouds and colors of the sky, the sea lions barking, and all the bird life. It's great to sit back after a hard day of working on the lighthouse and all the buildings and know that this is why we're here."

The historical significance of Cape St. Elias is by no means lost on the Boccis, however. This is especially true for Toni, who hails from a family of commercial fishermen. "My grandfather fished, my father fished, and they always came home safely," she says. "A lot of that was because of the lights."

Sea lion rookery, Cape St. Elias

"The history of the Cape St. Elias Station is very alluring," she says. "There are old photographs of Ted Pederson here at the cape in his [U.S. Lighthouse Service] hat and uniform. You can imagine him climbing all those stairs to the cupola, lighting the lamp, opening the vents, and raising the vent ball to make sure the light was there for the mariners."

One of Alaska's best known and remembered lighthouse personalities, Pederson was born in the Aleutians in 1905. The son of an Arctic whaler, he was part Russian, part Aleut, and Alaskan through and through. Pederson arrived at Cape St. Elias in 1927 to serve as the station's third assistant keeper. Two years later he was transferred to the light station at Cape Sarichef on Unimak Island in the Aleutians, which, if such can be imagined, was even more remote than Cape St. Elias. There he replaced a station crew member who had been driven to the point of insanity by the isolation.

Pederson seemed impervious to loneliness. In fact, he relished his new assignment at Cape Sarichef, which allowed him plenty of time to hunt, fish, and enjoy the wild country. He was no hermit, however. In 1934 Pederson learned that a single woman was teaching school at a small fishing community on the opposite side of the island. Although it was the dead of winter, he hiked more than 260 miles around the circumference of the island just to meet her. As it happened, she did not like him. So he turned around and hiked back to his station.

Later Pederson served at lighthouses in California, a much warmer state, but not as much to his liking. After the Coast Guard absorbed the

Ted Pederson served at some of Alaska's most remote light stations including **Cape St. Elias** where this photograph was taken in 1927.

Lighthouse Service in 1939, Pederson decided to go his own way and returned to Alaska as a homesteader. He died in 1990, having lived out the last half century of his life on the shores of Bear Cove near the head of Kachemak Bay.

Like Pederson, Bill Tinsley once served as an assistant keeper at the St. Elias Lighthouse. Posted here by the Coast Guard during World War II, he spent fourteen months at the cold, lonely island station. "I thought it was the last place on earth," says Tinsley. "There was no leaving the island, no getting off. We were supposed to get mail and supplies once a month, but the Coast Guard was busy with the war, busy doing other things. We were lucky if we got mail every two months."

Tinsley and his fellow keepers watched not just for Coast Guard tenders but for enemy ships that might launch a raid on their station. As it turned out, the only enemies they would

Former lighthouse keeper Bill Tinsley

fight were boredom and Alaska's legendary bad weather. "When there was a gale from the southeast, the snow would stick to the glass of the lantern room," says Tinsley. "We would be up here hour after hour scraping, cleaning, and hoping the wind would stop so we could get down off the tower and get warm."

Once the snow had piled up on the ground, it provided the young coastguardsmen with a way to break the monotony. They cleared themselves a ski run and fashioned makeshift skis from wooden planks, boiled so that the tips could be turned upward. "We'd have contests to see who could ski the farthest out toward the beach," says Tinsley. "After a while, I thought I should be going to the Olympics."

Tinsley never made it to the Olympics, but after a very long time—fifty-eight years, in fact—he did make it back to Cape St. Elias. During the summer of 2000, as part of the *Legendary Lighthouses* PBS documentary production, he returned to Kayak Island to have a look at his old duty station.

"Cape, I'm home."

"Cape, I'm home," said Bill Tinsley. "Long time no see."

Walking through the nearly empty lighthouse, Tinsley found much that was familiar to him. He visited the personal quarters where he had slept for fourteen months; the lantern room, which in his day had held a massive prismatic lens; and the communications room that once housed the station's all-important shortwave radio. For months at a time the radio had provided Tinsley and the other keepers their only contact with the outside world.

"Of course, in 1942 and 1943 all of this was in much better shape," he said. "The poor old place certainly has deteriorated. Still my being out here right now is one of the biggest thrills of my life. I can enjoy it now more than I did back then because I know I don't have to spend fourteen months out here. I can leave any time I want and go back home."

Of Gold Strikes and Ghost Ships

Alaska—the land of the eagle, the bear, the wolf, and the caribou. It exerts an almost magical pull on Americans. Its very mention brings to mind images of soul-expanding scenery—mighty rivers, towering mountain ranges, giant glaciers, tall forests, and endless expanses of tundra. It sparks in us a longing for wide open spaces and adventure, for Alaska is America's last true wilderness, our final frontier. In our imaginations Alaska is always there, waiting for us to stake our claims and either make our fortunes or go bust, as so many have done before.

Alaska—the land of the bear

But the grandeur of wilderness scenery held little attraction for many of Alaska's early immigrants. They came looking for gold. Prospectors swarmed into Alaska and the Yukon during a series of gold rushes or "stampedes" beginning in the late 1800s and lasting until about 1910. Only a tiny fraction of them would strike it rich, and more than a few would pay with their lives for their north country adventures. Some never even reached the gold fields. Jammed with steamers headed for the coastal boom towns of Juneau and Skagway, Alaska's dark, poorly charted waterways exacted a grim toll of vessels and their passengers.

For decades following the purchase of Alaska from the Russians in 1867, the U.S. government put little effort into making this vast new territory safe for navigation. The cost of building and maintaining even a limited system of lights along Alaska's extraordinarily remote and rugged coast was considered prohibitive. But this attitude began to change in 1896 when a major gold strike in Canada's Klondike region touched off a wild northward rush of treasure seekers.

During the Klondike Gold Rush, fragile steamers like this one cut through Alaska's dangerous coastal waters to supply the mining camps. More than a few were lost along with hundreds of prospectors and fortunes in gold dust. Most of Alaska's lighthouses were built during, or just after, the gold rush.

The three-fold increase in shipping traffic generated by the strikes brought with it a rash of shipwrecks, especially along the Inside Passage used by most stampeders to reach the Klondike. Rocks, ice, and blizzards claimed many vessels, such as the *Clara Nevada* lost near Eldred Rock in 1898. Driven onto the rock by hurricane-force winds, the hapless steamer ripped open her hull and went to the bottom, carrying down with her a large shipment of dynamite, $100,000 worth of Klondike gold dust, and about one hundred miners. In 1901 the gold-laden *Islander* struck an iceberg off Douglass Island and sank, along with forty-two passengers and crew.

Faced with losses of this scale, Congress finally began to appropriate funds to build lighthouses in Alaska. By the end of 1902 key light stations were in operation on Five Finger Island and Sentinel Island in the Inside Passage. Other stations, such as those at Tree Point, Mary Island, Point Retreat, and Cape Sarichef, soon followed. Ironically the Klondike Stampede had ended long before most of these lighthouses were built. Eldred Rock received a lighthouse in 1906—several years too late to assist the *Clara Nevada*.

Even with lights in place, Alaska's waters could be—and remain to this day—quite dangerous. In May 1910 the steamer *Princess May* ran aground on the north end of Sentinel

Island—within sight of the lighthouse. Only eight years afterwards one of the worst maritime disasters in American history took place just north of the same island light station when the *Princess Sophia* ran onto the rocks of Vanderbilt Reef in the teeth of an October blizzard. Although the lighthouse tender *Cedar* waited nearby in the protective lee of Sentinel Island, 100-mile-per-hour winds prevented it from rescuing the stricken steamer's 343 passengers and crew. The *Princess Sophia* remained in the deadly grip of the reef for more than twenty-four agonizing hours, then slipped off the rocks and plunged into the icy depths. There were no survivors. News of this 1918 disaster, which came just weeks after the end of World War I, shocked a world already numbed by four long years of battlefield carnage.

A Dangerous Coast with Few Lighthouses

Alaska is called the Great Land for good reason. Measuring 2,400 miles from east to west and 1,400 miles from north to south, our nation's forty-ninth state encompasses nearly 400 million acres, which makes it larger than many entire nations. That's a lot of land. But the land is only part of the Alaskan story. Water also has an important role to play.

Those who know little of Alaska or its people may be surprised to learn that it is heavily dependent on coastal shipping for transportation and its very economic survival. There are few roads, and travel to the interior can be quite difficult, not just in winter, but in any season. Not surprisingly, many of Alaska's cities and towns are located on the coast, where liquid highways can take the place of roads.

"Alaska really depends on the oceans," says David Benton, one of the founders of the Alaska Lighthouse Association. "Alaska was discovered by way of the ocean, and virtually everyone and everything comes here by sea."

The coast of Alaska is longer than that of all the rest of the United States combined. Counting all

David Benton

THE INSIDE PASSAGE

Often called the Alaskan panhandle, the state's southeastern region consists of a narrow strip of mainland and a 500-mile-long chain of coastal islands extending from the Gulf of Alaska southward to the Canadian boundary waters just north of Prince Rupert, British Columbia. The ocean has blessed the panhandle with relatively mild temperatures, but the extremely rugged geography has left very little room for people. The few small cities and towns such as Ketchikan, Wrangell, Petersburg, and Juneau—the state capital—are hemmed in by mountains, ice fields, and dense rain forests. There are almost no roads. Water is the lifeline for these southeastern communities.

A bird's-eye view of the **Eldred Rock Lighthouse**

Fortunately for those who live here and for the hundreds of thousands of tourists who visit the area each year, water transportation is readily accessible. The panhandle's long, mountainous islands protect a maze of inlets, straits, sounds, and other navigable waterways. Threading its way through this saltwater labyrinth is a series of interconnected shipping lanes and channels known collectively as the Inside Passage. Ferries, passenger liners, and freighters regularly ply the Inside Passage, which ranges from 30 miles to only about 300 yards in width.

For tourists the Inside Passage provides access to a natural wonderland teeming with wildlife. The spectacular scenery includes towering peaks, hanging glaciers, icebergs, dark green coniferous forests, and an almost endless array of ocean and mountain vistas. The old Russian settlement of Sitka and other quaint panhandle communities delight visitors with their frontier ambience. There are also a number of historic lighthouses along the passage, and these, of course, add to its charm.

The Inside Passage is not just an Alaskan waterway: It stretches all the way along the British Columbian coast and into Washington state as far as Bellingham just north of Seattle. Some who travel the Inside Passage choose to board passenger liners or ferries departing from Bellingham. The Alaska Marine Highway ferry Columbia makes regularly scheduled runs from Bellingham to Skagway at the far northern end of the Inside Passage. Cruise liners from as far away as Honolulu and San Diego also frequent the passage.

its bays, fjords, inlets, passages, and estuaries, it has nearly 34,000 miles of shore, about thirty times as much as California. Much of this incredibly extensive shoreline is as wild as Alaska's untamed interior. Strewn with rocks, perennially cloaked in fog, and frequently blasted by ferocious storms, the waters off Alaska are among the most treacherous on earth. Yet despite these dangers and the extraordinary length of its coast, Alaska can boast only eleven lighthouses, about the same number that guard Cape Cod.

"These lighthouses were put here to open up the country," says Benton. "They are an important part of our history and they are important right now."

Although few in number, Alaska's lighthouses are vital to the freighters, ferries, and passenger liners that keep the state's economy humming. "People depend on them just as they did a hundred years ago," Benton says.

Lighthouses were always scarce in Alaska, largely because they were so difficult to build and maintain. Materials had to be shipped 1,000 miles or more from the lower states to construction sites so remote that they might be several days' sail from the nearest small port. Laborers had to live full-time at the site, contending with extreme weather, dangerous animals, and meager rations until the light tower stood tall and the job was finished.

Once a light station was completed, it could be staffed only by keepers willing to live for months, if not years, in complete isolation. A tour of duty at an Alaska lighthouse was seldom less than nine months and in some cases as much as three years. Supply vessels might visit remote stations only once a year. Alaska's keepers, like the trappers and woodsmen of the interior, became legendary for their ability to endure hardship and solitude. Some died in the line of duty, the victims of cold, disease, or natural disaster.

Nowadays Alaska's lighthouses no longer have resident keepers. As with light stations throughout the United States, all those in Alaska have been automated. The lonely sentinels continue to do their work of guiding mariners and warning them away from navigational obstacles, but the towers and keepers' quarters stand empty and silent. Without full-time keepers and other station personnel to paint walls, polish brass, replace broken windows, and patch roofs, the old light stations have suffered. While the Coast Guard keeps the lights faithfully burning, station buildings have been left more or less at the mercy of the elements.

"These lighthouses represent a wonderful maritime history," says Alaska historian Joseph Leahy. "If the structures are allowed to deteriorate, it damages that history."

Joe Leahy

Fortunately the plight of Alaska's light stations has given rise to a new variety of lighthouse keeper. Mindful of the need to preserve important reminders of a rich maritime heritage, Alaskans are coming to the aid of their lighthouses.

Traffic Light on Admiralty Island

L ocated at the northern tip of Admiralty Island, Point Retreat overlooks a busy maritime intersection where freighters, ferries, and passenger liners often cross paths. Here key shipping channels converge to link the capital city of Juneau with the Inside Passage and the rest of southeastern Alaska. As one might expect, this watery crossroads is marked by a navigational beacon.

Established in 1904, the Point Retreat Light Station has been guiding mariners for almost a century. For much of that time the station's all important navigational light was focused by a giant Fresnel lens located on top of a relatively short 25-foot tower. Shaped something like a clamshell, the heavy prismatic glass lens was rotated by machinery, and it produced a flashing light that could be seen from many miles away. When the range of the light was limited by foul weather, it got an assist from a throaty fog signal powered by engines housed in a concrete structure beneath the tower.

Point Retreat Lighthouse, Admiralty Island

Lew Daniels

All this equipment required constant attention, and teams of up to six keepers once lived here working in round-the-clock shifts to keep it running. One of those who served at Point Retreat was Lew Daniels, who came here as a young Coast Guard recruit on his first assignment. Daniels had volunteered for this remote post in order to take advantage of a special inducement offered to anyone willing to put up with the isolation of lighthouse duty—three months leave at the end of a twelve-month stint.

"I remember the very date I arrived," says Daniels, now retired. "It was December 14, 1943."

Daniels found Point Retreat less lonely than he had expected. There was a family—the station commander, his wife, and their small child—and Daniels shared his day-to-day life and work with five other coastguardsmen. His job was to watch over the two sizable diesel motors that drove the fog signal and generated the electric power needed to light up the station's huge Fresnel lens—what Daniels called "the big globe up in the tower." He took the midnight to 8:00 A.M. watch—often referred to as the graveyard shift. These

The **Point Retreat Lighthouse** sits at the confluence of two shipping channels in southeast Alaska's vast maze of islands and waterways known as "The Inside Passage." More maritime traffic passes Point Retreat than any other Alaskan lighthouse. It is located at the northern tip of the hundred-mile-long Admiralty Island, a wilderness rain forest that is home to the greatest known concentration of brown bears and nesting bald eagles in the world.

early work hours would have been unattractive to most, but Daniels liked his upside-down schedule. It allowed him to sleep during the day and socialize with the other keepers during the evening.

No doubt the Point Retreat keepers shared their off-duty hours in much the way servicemen do everywhere. They exchanged stories, told jokes, and played cards. Daniels discovered that he had a knack for poker.

"Mostly we played draw poker or five-card stud. I must have been lucky because the guys stopped playing with me."

Banned from the card table, Daniels took up fishing and found that he was also lucky at that. "I caught the first fish of my life—a forty-five-pound salmon," Daniels says. "Then I caught an eighty-nine-pound halibut. Now that was exciting."

When Daniels's twelve month stay at Point Retreat was over, he took his ninety-day leave and then moved on to assignments at other Coast Guard installations. Although Daniels never forgot the friends he had made and the unique experiences he had enjoyed there, he would not see Point Retreat again for fifty-five years. Then in 1998, during a family outing to Alaska, he paid the old light station a visit. He was treated to a special tour of the place by David Benton, who now leases the property from the Coast Guard.

In many ways Point Retreat was not as Daniels remembered it. The big lens that had once lighted the way for mariners was gone, along with the hefty engines he himself had once operated. Most of the station structures now stood empty, and there were no Coast Guard personnel on hand to keep everything shipshape as they had in Daniels's day.

Most of these changes date to the 1970s when Point Retreat and several other Alaska lighthouses were automated. To save labor and expense, the Coast Guard removed the station's Fresnel lens, replacing it with a small, though powerful, aeromarine optic requiring little or no maintenance. An automated system replaced the original fog signal machinery as well. Soon afterwards the station's last keepers packed their bags and headed for the mainland, leaving the buildings at Point Retreat silent, empty, and more or less neglected.

Daniels, however, was happy to learn that now, more than a quarter century since the station was automated, voices and laughter are once more heard at Point Retreat. So too are the sounds of hammers and drills. The people who come here—mostly on weekends during the warmer weather months—are not sent here by the Coast Guard. Nor are they lighthouse keepers in the traditional sense. Rather, they are keepers of a historic property, a reminder of Alaska's maritime past. Most are members of the Alaska Lighthouse Association.

Dave Benton helps guide the association's efforts at Point Retreat. For fourteen years Benton served as Alaska's international fisheries negotiator, but recently he gave up that high level position for a different job—one much closer to the earth and water. Now he devotes much of his time to the hard but emotionally rewarding task of restoring the Point Retreat Lighthouse to its former glory.

Volunteers replace sidewalk at Point Retreat Lighthouse.

With help from association volunteers Benton is struggling to rebuild the station's infrastructure. "When the Coast Guard decommissioned the light station in 1973, they pulled everything out of here," says Benton. "They pulled out the electrical system, the water system, the sewer system—everything. Right now we're putting back the basic utilities, stabilizing buildings, painting walls, and replacing rotten walkways."

The work is not easy, and Benton admits there are problems. For instance, getting supplies and equipment to the site is always time-consuming and difficult. "It's about 17 miles from Juneau to Point Retreat, and we haul everything out here in a skiff and a fishing boat. It's a chore pulling heavy stuff 45 or maybe 50 feet up from the pier to the top of the dock, but it's also a lot of fun."

In time Benton and his friends hope to put Point Retreat back on an operational footing, not as an official Coast Guard light station, but as a maritime history museum. "We want people to come out here and get a sense of the history and of what went on when this country opened up. Lighthouses like this one reflect that. They played a unique role in that, and they still play a role in the maritime culture of Alaska. Even today, you come out here in winter in the freezing spray and with the winds blowing 80 or 90 miles an hour, and it's kind of nice to know there's a lighthouse telling you you're not going to run up on the rocks. This place, we hope, is going to help people understand that."

Nature will be an important part of the Point Retreat experience. "We've got a whole lot of wildlife out here," says Benton. "We've got deer, mink, owls, eagle, ravens, peregrine falcons, and once in a while, a few brown bears. In the marine environment we've got humpback whales, orcas, sea lions, harbor seals, and otters. It's really a phenomenal place to sit and watch animals."

The Five Fingers of Frederick Sound

About 80 miles south of Point Retreat another historic Alaskan light station is being restored. Known as the Five Finger Islands Lighthouse, it is located on a long slender scrap of rock rising from the crystal waters of Frederick Sound to the north of Petersburg. Its white deco-style tower is a familiar sight to passengers on ferries, luxury liners, and tour boats moving up and down Alaska's extraordinarily scenic Inside Passage.

Five Finger Islands Lighthouse clings to a blade of rock in Frederick Sound. Like all of Alaska's lighthouses, the structure at Five Finger Islands is not accessible by car. Passengers on Alaska's many cruise ships often have the best view of this light.

The Juneau Lighthouse Association has leased the **Five Finger Islands Lighthouse** for use as a research center, but supplying it is no easy task.

Travelers passing through Frederick Sound may delight in their view of the lighthouse clinging to its stony islet, but there are many other marvels to compete with it. Most are natural wonders, rather than man-made ones. Like much of the Alaskan coast and the 1,000-mile-long Inside Passage, Frederick Sound is a naturalist's paradise. Here forest-cloaked mountains rise on all sides while icebergs calved from immense glaciers on the mainland shimmer in the distance. Trees along the shoreline are often crowned with bald eagles keeping watch for schools of large fish. During the summer humpback whales roil the surface and throw their huge tails in the air before diving to avoid approaching vessels. The humpbacks are true giants, growing up to 52 feet in length and weighing as much as fifty tons. Their tongues alone may weigh as much as 4,000 pounds.

To study the abundant wildlife of the sound, the Juneau Lighthouse Association has leased the Five Finger Islands Lighthouse for use as an offshore whale-watching and research center. Founded by Michael and Valerie O'Hare, Ed McIntosh, and Jennifer Klein, four friends interested in nature and maritime history, the association applied for one of the lighthouse leases offered by the U.S. Coast Guard during the late 1990s. Competition for the leases was fierce, with as many as 500 applicants vying for each of the available lighthouse properties, but the government administrators in charge of the leasing program thought highly of the Juneau Association proposal to use the old station as a nature center. Ultimately, after a series of group interviews with the members, the association got the lease.

"It was like winning the lottery," says O'Hare.

Along with the lease came an enormous responsibility, however, and a lot of work. Automated in 1984, Five Fingers Island was the last of Alaska's light stations to be decommissioned by the Coast Guard, and it remains in relatively good condition. Even so, the old station needed plenty of help when the association took charge in 1998. Concrete walls had begun to crack, pipes had frozen and burst, and the whole place cried out for paint. But while the job facing them was a substantial one, association members have shouldered it energetically. After all, restoration and maintenance are a key requirement of their lease.

Ed McIntosh

To work on the station, members must commute some 65 miles from Juneau by way of a small boat or, on occasion, by floatplane. Money is not always available for necessary materials, equipment, and supplies. Despite the problems, however, substantial progress has been made.

"We've got running water, electricity, and sewers," says the mechanically minded Ed McIntosh, considered a veritable Mr. Fixit by other less handy association members. "We've still got a million things to do, but it's livable. The lighthouse still needs a lot of paint and a lot of repair, but we've stopped it from deteriorating."

Even the station's brass work is once again receiving attention. "One of my favorite chores is polishing the brass," says Jennifer Klein. "When there was a Coast Guard crew here,

they polished the brass and had chores they did every day. That's what kept the lighthouse together. If I can get it back to the state it was in when it was actually an open lighthouse, then I feel like I've accomplished something."

By patching pipes, painting walls, polishing brass, or taking care of a host of other station tasks, association members follow in the footsteps of generations of keepers who served here. Five Finger Islands Light Station has a long and venerable history, dating back to Alaska's gold rush years when passenger steamers loaded with mules and prospectors crowded the Inside Passage. Completed early in 1902, it was the first government lighthouse to be built in Alaska. The original two-story

Keeping a historic light station in tip-top condition takes a lot of work. The brass rails of the tower stairway at **Five Finger Islands** require frequent polishing.

The breathtaking view of Frederick Sound from the lantern room is one of the rewards for volunteers working at **Five Finger Islands Lighthouse**. Volunteers often endure a four-hour boat trip from Juneau to reach the light.

combination tower and residence was a Victorian-style wooden structure with a small lantern room perched on its roof. It displayed a fixed white light focused by a fourth-order Fresnel lens. Just as it does today, the beacon guided vessels into the strategic channel west of Admiralty Island. It also warned them away from the treacherous fingerlike islands for which the station was named.

"Mariners in this area said the islands looked like a hand reaching up to pull them down," says O'Hare.

No doubt the Five Finger Islands Lighthouse prevented many wrecks and saved numerous lives. Ironically the original lighthouse itself was pulled down by disaster in December 1933, when fire leveled both tower and dwelling. The bitter cold had frozen the station's pipes, and one of the keepers was trying to thaw them out with a blowtorch. The heat ignited the tender dry walls, and soon the entire structure was engulfed in flames.

John Leadbetter, captain of the lighthouse tender *Cedar*, had just come ashore with a load of supplies when the accident happened. Leadbetter watched in amazement as keeper Nicholas Kashevaroff plunged into the burning building to save the station's logbook. Moments later Kashevaroff emerged, clutching a large volume. But when the singed keeper looked down at it, he discovered that, instead of the logbook, he had rescued a Sears, Roebuck catalog.

Built in 1902, the original **Five Finger Islands Lighthouse** was Alaska's first government navigational station. Burned in 1933, it was soon replaced by this reinforced-concrete structure. The rather stark art deco styling is typical of Alaskan lighthouses.

Young bald eagle lacking the white head feathers typical of adults.

Valerie and Michael O'Hare

"Well," said Captain Leadbetter, "I see you got the place warmed up."

Within two years the incinerated lighthouse had been replaced by the reinforced-concrete edifice that still stands today. Erected atop a hefty concrete pier, it was completed and in operation by late 1935. The main building, which served as a platform for the 68-foot tower, was only 40 feet square. Keepers shared the limited interior spaces with a jumble of boilers, batteries, and other equipment. Now most of the equipment is gone along with the Coast Guard personnel, but for nearly half a century keepers lived here full time for a year or more at a stretch. For them the lighthouse and its three-acre island must have seemed very small indeed.

For the current keepers, however, this place is in no way confining. Members of the Juneau Lighthouse Association regard Five Fingers Island as a window on a vast natural world.

"We have a lot of whales here," says Jennifer Klein. "We have Dall porpoises and Steller sea lions. It's amazing the life we have on this little three-acre island. There's fireweed in brilliant magenta. You can see dogwood. And when we arrived this spring, we were surprised to find an eagle's nest."

Klein and her fellow association members hope to make the island and its wonders more accessible to the public. "Whatever happens, people are going to be welcome here," Klein says.

North to Alaska

Every year the magic of Alaska's southeastern coast attracts thousands of visitors. Most arrive on one of the large and luxurious cruise liners that frequent the state's spectacular coast. But a few choose to come by way of the state-run ferries *Taku*, *Columbia*, *Matanuska*, *Kennicott*, and *Aurora* that regularly ply the relatively calm waters of the Inside Passage. A ferry trip from Bellingham, Washington, to Skagway at the far northern end of the Passage can take up to four days, but the time passes fast. In warm weather passengers crowd the rails to enjoy the amazingly beautiful scenery or to watch for whales and other sea life.

Tamara Fewell-Flowers has a job that anyone who loves water and nature would envy. She is one of the U.S. Forest Service interpreters who ride the ferries of the Alaska Marine Highway System. She teaches passengers about Alaska's coastal waters, rain forests, wildlife, history, geography—and lighthouses.

"For a lot of people Alaska is the last frontier," says Fewell-Flowers. "The magnitude of the scenery—the ocean, the mountains, and the forest—can be overwhelming."

Passengers often ask about lighthouses along the Inside Passage. "Today there are nine lighthouses that mark the Passage," says Fewell-Flowers. "Lighthouses are still really important here, especially for our small boat operators and fishermen."

Ferries traveling northward from British Columbia cross over into U.S. waters about halfway between Prince Rupert and Ketchikan. As with most of the Alaskan coast, the shoreline just north of the border is undeveloped and wild. The first man-made structure northbound passengers are likely to see in Alaska is a lighthouse.

"Tree Point is Alaska's southernmost lighthouse," says Fewell-Flowers. "Tree Point marks the gateway to the Inside Passage. It is the first lighthouse mariners see as they enter U.S. waters."

Established in 1903, the Tree Point Light Station has served mariners for nearly a century. The concrete, deco-style tower seen today was built in 1935, when it replaced an earlier wooden structure. Originally the station's beacon was focused by a fourth-order Fresnel lens, but that was removed after the station was automated in 1969. The old lens can now be seen at the Tongass Historical Museum in Ketchikan.

Alaska State Ferry

Tamara Fewell-Flowers, U.S. Forest Service Interpreter

Tower at Tree Point Light Station

Until 1969 the station's light and fog signal required the care of full-time keepers who lived at Tree Point year-round. As with other Alaskan light stations, Tree Point could not be reached by road, so the keepers and their families lived a secluded existence.

Now abandoned, this wooden residence was home to generations of keepers at secluded **Tree Point,** Alaska's southernmost lighthouse. Supplies delivered by tender were loaded onto carts and brought to the house on the tramway still visible on the right.

"It was very isolated here, but we loved it," says Angelina Salvato, who came to Tree Point in 1947 with her husband and their two children.

The keepers and their families did not live in the main lighthouse building, but in separate nearby residences. "These houses were beautiful," says Salvato. "There were two bedrooms downstairs, a living room, and a really nice kitchen with a lot of cupboard space."

Angelina Salvato

Occasionally Salvato's housekeeping received a special impetus unknown to most homemakers. Coast Guard inspectors paid regular visits to the Tree Point facility, and not even the keepers' homes escaped their scrutiny. "These houses were inspected all the time," says Salvato. "The Coast Guard officers would come in with their white gloves and see if I'd left any dust. But mine was clean. I always got the OK."

Supplies had to be brought in from Ketchikan about 50 miles to the north, so pantries were kept well stocked. "I had a complete grocery store downstairs," says Salvato. "I had fifty pounds of butter. I made all my cookies with butter. I had to make my own homemade bread, but of course, I had the time. There was no place to go."

Despite the isolation the Salvato family found plenty to keep them busy. "We went trapping for mink and sold them to Sears and Roebuck," says Salvato. "And we went fishing. I caught a 125-pound halibut. I was pregnant at the time, and my husband couldn't believe the fish I had caught. I sold it to a fish buyer for $11 and bought a nice pair of shoes with the money."

Good Old Days on the Inside Passage

The next lighthouse up the line from Tree Point is located on Mary Island, approximately twenty miles south of Ketchikan. The Tree Point beacon marks a key waterway with a tongue twisting name—the Revillagigedo Channel. In 1937 a 61-foot concrete tower replaced the wooden lighthouse that had been erected in 1903. The light atop the tower still guides mariners.

Captain Larry Walters watches for the Mary Island beacon when he is in these waters. Captain Walters is master of the *Aurora*, one of the ferries that serves the Alaska Marine Highway System. "There are some unique navigational perils in southeast Alaska," says Captain Walters. "Many of the channels are like Norwegian fjords. They're deep, but narrow and long. And we have numerous rocks, reefs, and shoals."

Larry Walters plotting a course through the Inside Passage.

Because many places in Alaska are accessible only by boat or airplane, the Alaska Marine Highway System is a key transportation link. This is especially true in southeast Alaska along the Inside Passage, a protected waterway that runs from Seattle, Washington, to Skagway, Alaska. Not surprisingly, most of Alaska's lighthouses were built through the waterway; they date from the late 1800s, when the Klondike gold rush dramatically increased shipping traffic through the Inside Passage.

Along most of America's coasts, lighthouses have lost much of their usefulness to navigation. With the help of sophisticated electronics, mariners can pinpoint their positions without the aid of beacons. In Alaska, however, the lights still make an important contribution to navigational safety.

Like other navigators nowadays, Captain Walters relies primarily on radar. "But here in southeastern Alaska we always check our position using a lighthouse, a buoy, or a lighted aide," he says. "We take visual bearings much as was done a hundred years ago. Lighthouses help us establish our position and find the next point of land," he says.

During the first few decades of the twentieth century, lighthouses were not just helpful, but essential to the captains, pilots, and navigators braving Alaska's hazardous waters. Despite the dangers they faced, however, many old-time mariners look back on this period fondly. So too does Baard Lervick, a retired general foreman who joined the civilian Lighthouse Service before it was taken over by the U.S. Coast Guard in 1939.

"They didn't have electricity on boats in the good old days," says Lervick. "They had no radios, no radio beacons. They depended on the light, and when it was foggy they depended on the fog horn."

Lervick lived through the last years of the period he describes as "the good old days" during his childhood, much of which was spent at the Mary Island Lighthouse. His father was appointed keeper of the light in 1922. "We came here from Tree Point when I was five years old or four and three-quarters or

Another art deco–style structure, the **Mary Island Lighthouse** dates to 1937 when it replaced an earlier wooden lighthouse. The Mary Island tower was built to guide ships between Tree Point and Ketchikan.

something like that," says Lervick. "We stayed until I was twelve, when my father was promoted to depot keeper at Ketchikan."

For years the remote Mary Island station had no electricity. The fourth-order Fresnel lens at the top of the wooden tower received its light from a chemically fueled lamp with a delicate mantle. At night the nearby keeper's residence was lit with kerosene lamps. Then in 1927 batteries were installed in the tower and the lantern was fitted with electric bulbs. Even so, Lervick's family could enjoy the benefits of electricity only when the generators were recharging the station's sixty-five glass-lined batteries. "The women had to do their ironing or whatever when the generators were running."

But Lervick didn't mind living under what many would have considered rustic circumstances. "We had a whole island to explore," he says. "In the summertime we went swimming once, twice, maybe three times a day. I had a skiff, and I went trolling for salmon. I used to catch some pretty good fish."

Eventually Lervick followed his father's example and joined the Lighthouse Service. He worked first at the Scotch Cap Lighthouse in the Aleutian Islands and then at the Tree Point Light Station. Later he served as keeper of the Mary Island Lighthouse, where he had spent his formative years.

A Sparkling Chain

Northbound Alaska ferries nearly always make their first stop at Ketchikan, known to many as the rainiest place in America. Its soggy weather station measures an average of 162 inches (13½ feet) of precipitation a year. The locals tend to ignore the constant drizzle and frequent downpours. Visitors, on the other hand, may want to bring their umbrellas, but they'll find there is a lot more to Ketchikan than rain. This vigorous lumbering and fishing community is alive with a true frontier spirit.

Ketchikan has a population of 8,000, which by Alaskan standards makes it quite a large town. The comings and goings of passenger liners, ferries, fishing boats, and floatplanes give the impression of a bustling hub. Travelers who choose to stay for a while will want to stop by the Totem Heritage Center to see some fine examples of the region's trademark indigenous art. At the Tongass Historical Museum they will find what many might also consider a work of art—the old third-order Fresnel lens from the Tree Point Lighthouse.

Ferries moving up the Inside Passage from Ketchikan encounter many navigational lights, but very few are lighthouses. Most of the guiding beacons along the Inside Passage are light buoys or pole lights located on or near the shore. The most impressive array of naviga-

Because they require constant maintenance, the sparkling Fresnel lenses that once focused the beacons of Alaska's lighthouses have been removed. Most of the big, chandelierlike glass lenses have been given to museums where they can be seen and enjoyed by the public. The Cape Spencer lens, for example, is now on display at a museum in Juneau.

The aeromarine beacons and Vega lights that took the place of these lenses do an efficient job of lighting the coast and guiding mariners. Inexpensive and easy to repair or replace, these modern optics make sense in a region where lighthouses may be hundreds of miles from the nearest town. Interestingly, however, the new optics are little more effective than the Fresnel lenses they replaced.

Invented in 1822 by French physicist Augustin Fresnel, the prismatic Fresnel lens was long considered the most sophisticated technology available for focusing a navigational light. For more than a century and a half it was standard equipment in lighthouses all over the world.

"Fresnel devised a system for bending light and concentrating it into a single, strong beam," says Alaska lighthouse historian Joe Leahy.

The Cape Spencer lens, for instance, had four bull's eyes, each of which focused the light of the station's lamps into a powerful beam. As the lens was rotated by machinery in the tower, the beams turned like the spokes of a giant wheel. A mariner in a ship 10 or 20 miles away would see the beam just briefly and recognize it as a flash. Modern electric optics accomplish the same effect by blinking on and off.

Although a Fresnel lens appears to be a single piece of molded glass, it actually consists of many separate prisms. As many as a thousand or as few as twenty individual pieces of glass may be fitted into the metal frame of a Fresnel lens. This makes the lenses very delicate and extremely difficult to break down and reassemble.

"There is no road map to show you how to put these things together," says Leahy. "You have to understand how they were built. If you look at the corners where four pieces come together, you'll see there is a number for each piece. That's the only guide to assembling these lenses."

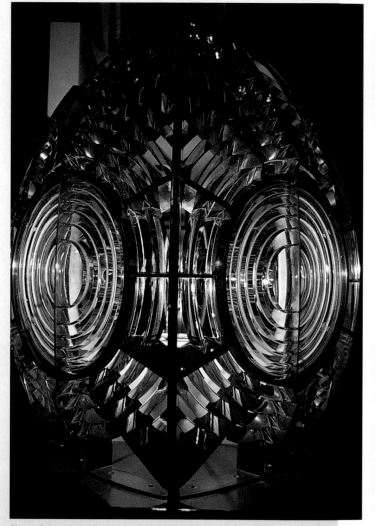

None of the original Fresnel lenses remain in any of Alaska's lighthouses. **Cape Spencer's** lens is on display at the Alaska State Museum in Juneau. Others are preserved in local museums.

Some are calling on the Coast Guard to return the historic lenses to the lighthouse where they once served. "I think we would all prefer to see the lenses in the lighthouses," Leahy says. "But in Alaska, that's difficult. There are no lighthouses in Alaska that you can drive to. The best opportunity to see and appreciate the lenses and learn about the maritime history is in the community museums."

tional lights in Alaska, or perhaps anywhere, marks the southern approach to Petersburg, located about 120 miles north of Ketchikan. A busy fishing community with a strong Norwegian heritage, Petersburg is reached by northbound vessels via the Wrangell Narrows. More than 20 miles long and only 300 feet wide in places, this dramatic waterway is marked by a sparkling chain of red, green, and white channel lights. Ferries often thread their way through the serpentine narrows channel very late in the evening. They are guided by the lights glittering like gems along a dark shore, which looms so close in places that you can almost lean out from the rail and touch the limbs of trees. Passengers who can stay awake long enough to witness this adventure will experience a night to remember.

Sentinel at the Door

More than 100 miles north of Petersburg, near Point Retreat, ferries round Admiralty Island and turn toward Juneau. Like Ketchikan, this old gold-mining town throbs with activity. It is, after all, the state capital and, with more than 30,000 residents, by far the largest community in southeastern Alaska.

The only waterlocked capital city in the United States, Juneau is walled in by mountains and the sea. While Juneau cannot be reached by road, it receives a steady stream of visitors who arrive by air, cruise liner, and ferry. Although cruise ships often dock right in the middle of this lovely city, often described as "Little San Francisco," ferries must land at the Auke Bay Terminal about 14 miles north of town. As a result ferry passengers approaching the area won't see much of Juneau, but they may catch a glimpse of a lighthouse.

Located near the entrance to Auke Bay, the Sentinel Island Lighthouse has been guiding vessels to Juneau since 1902. Completed at a time when gold prospectors—Juneau is named for one of them—were still flocking to Alaska, the original lighthouse consisted of a wooden duplex dwelling with a central tower between the two sides. In 1935 the wooden tower was removed from the residence and a separate tower constructed nearby.

A poured-concrete structure about 50 feet high, the new tower was built in the stepped, thrusting art deco style typical of urban skyscrapers of the 1930s. Several of Alaska's existing lighthouses were built at about this time, and nearly all reflect similar design elements. One might think the modernist emphasis of art deco would be out of place in the wilds of Alaska, but oddly enough, these buildings seem an excellent complement to their surroundings. The stark white walls of the Sentinel Island tower, for example, present a breathtaking contrast to the emerald green of the forest background.

Located far from the nearest power lines, the **Sentinel Island Lighthouse** has been fitted with solar panels. During the day, they recharge the batteries that light the station's beacon at night.

Graced by a spectacular setting rivaling any in North America, this lighthouse stands against a backdrop not only of forest, but also of towering peaks and hanging glaciers. Resident keepers once enjoyed this setting, but no more. The dwelling where they lived a bucolic and solitary existence for a year or more at a time was demolished after the light was automated in 1966. Although the light remains in operation, it no longer needs human assistance. As with most other Alaskan navigational stations, solar panels help charge the batteries that supply electric power for the light and fog signal.

While Sentinel Island could be described as a lonely place, it is far more accessible than most of Alaska's light stations. The lighthouse here is visible, not just from the decks of passing ferries and passenger liners, but also from Highway 7 on the nearby mainland. This makes it unique among Alaskan lighthouses. "Sentinel Island is the only lighthouse that's visible from the Alaskan road system," says Gary Gillette. "But it's on an island, so you can't drive to it."

Gillette is president of the Gastineau Channel Historical Society in Juneau. The society has worked to preserve several historical structures in the area and now leases this lighthouse from the Coast Guard. Gillette, along with fellow society member Renee Hughes, pays frequent visits to the property.

86

"We bring our powerboat out here at high tide," says Gillette. "Or if we want to stay overnight, we come out in our kayak."

Landing on the island in a kayak can be challenging, especially if the water is choppy. "When it's really rough, getting out of a kayak on these rocky ledges is real tricky," says Gillette. "So we look for good places to pull in, places behind rocks that kind of calm down the waves."

Getting on and off the island was a bit easier for the keepers who lived here before the station was automated. The wooden dock used for the station's watercraft still exists, but it's not much help to kayakers. "The dock was constructed in 1902, when the original lighthouse was built," Gillette says. "It had a boathouse, a winch, and a crane so they could actually lift their boats out of the water."

Gary Gillette and Renee Hughes arrive at Sentinel Lighthouse by kayak.

A nearby tram helped keepers unload their supplies. (Tramways consisting of iron rails laid down over railroad ties were a common feature of Alaska lighthouses.) Unfortunately it has deteriorated to the point that it can no longer be used. Pressure-treated wood has been placed between the tracks to create a convenient walkway. Gillette and Hughes use a small cart to pull their gear over the planks.

Gary Gilette pulls a cart along the restored tram walkway.

Bringing in sufficient food and supplies for even a brief stay can be a lot of work, but for Gillette and Hughes the experience of staying at the lighthouse makes all the effort worthwhile. "I've stayed out here for as long as eight days and hated the idea of having to go home," says Gillette. But he also recognizes that it's nice to have a choice, unlike the station's Lighthouse Service and Coast Guard keepers who lived here year-round regardless of the circumstances or the weather. "I can imagine that in the middle of the winter when the wind was howling at 100 miles an hour and there was no way you could get off if you wanted to, it could be tough."

Gillette and other society members have begun to open the station to the public. "We want to make this place more accessible so people can come out here and enjoy it," he says. "It's a fun place and we want to share it."

Gillette is especially fond of the tower and its cupola. "It's about 60 feet above the water so you get quite a commanding 360-degree view," he says. "On a sunny day you can see glaciers, mountains, and wildlife. But even on a day when we've got winds and rain dripping on the windows, it's still very romantic. It's a great place to hang out and sip a cup of tea."

Construction of the **Eldred Rock Lighthouse** was prompted by the sinking of the passenger ship *Clara Nevada* in 1898, and the consequent loss of some one hundred lives and more than $100,000 in Klondike gold dust. Surrounded by magnificent Alaskan scenery, Eldred Rock is the oldest original lighthouse in Alaska.

A Tree Grows on Eldred Rock

The final northward leg of the famed Inside Passage carries travelers through the spectacular Lynn Canal and onward to the small towns of Haines and Skagway. Each year thousands of summer tourists make this journey, just as countless gold rush prospectors did a century ago. Today, just as it has since 1906, the Eldred Rock Light helps vessels and their passengers reach Skagway in safety.

Built partly in response to the *Clara Nevada* tragedy, the station looks much as it did when it was completed nearly a century ago. The main building is an octagonal, two-story wooden structure with a 56-foot tower rising through its center. The lighthouse is perched on the summit of the nearly barren rock; from a distance it could be mistaken for a church.

"Personally I think Eldred Rock is the most beautiful lighthouse I have ever seen," says Cindy Jones, director of the Sheldon Museum in Haines, where the Eldred Rock Station's original third-order Fresnel lens is now on display. "I'm sure it's the most beautiful lighthouse in the world in the most beautiful setting in the world, and it needs to be preserved."

Gordon Huggins

Located not far from Haines, Eldred Rock had year-round resident keepers until 1973, when the station was automated. Since then the old lighthouse has stood its vigil alone. Although its beacon continues to guide mariners, the untended structure has begun to deteriorate.

Still, Jones and others in Haines are determined to save the old lighthouse. "People in Haines have a love affair with this lighthouse," she says. "We travel a lot, and whenever we travel south, take the ferry, or even our own boat, we pass by Eldred Rock. If it's preserved, then people can come here, learn the history, and see for themselves what a wonderful place this is."

For Gordon Huggins, now retired from the U.S. Coast Guard, Eldred Rock was not so much a "wonderful place" as it was the place he worked. Huggins was assigned to this station as an engine man in 1963.

"When I was at Eldred Rock thirty-seven years ago, the only thing here was just the rock and the

The Eldred Rock Lighthouse sits in the middle of the picturesque Inside Passage.

building," Huggins says. "They dropped me off and I kind of wondered where I was. I knew I was in the middle of nowhere and was going to be here for a year."

In Alaska Coast Guard lighthouse crewmen had to adjust to the isolation. "The only way you got off one of these places was to get sick or die," says Huggins. "You were here for twelve months, and that was it. So you had to get your mind set to it and do what you had to do. They had crews in the past at other light stations that had probably gone a little crazy from being isolated. But the crew at Eldred Rock was real good."

Crew members kept busy with their work and the station routine. "I was an engine man out here," says Huggins. "It was my job to maintain and operate all the equipment."

Of course the crewmen also had spare time, but they could have difficulty finding worthwhile ways to use it. After all, one could only do so much fishing. Huggins, for some reason, became fascinated by trees.

Gordon Huggins standing beside one of his Eldred Rock trees.

"When I came out here, there wasn't tree one," he says. "There had never been a tree on Eldred Rock. I was over on the beach [on the mainland] one day, and there were a couple of small trees. I pulled them up out of the ground and figured I'd bring them back and plant them over here. I didn't think they'd ever do anything. No way in my wildest dreams did I think they'd ever grow this big."

Riches from the Sea

The discovery of gold in the rivers and mountains of the far northwest led to a flurry of lighthouse construction along the Inside Passage. As it turned out, however, Alaska's coastal waters held natural riches even more valuable than gold—salmon, herring, and tuna in such prodigious quantities that fishing boats often spilled over with their catch. The safe harvest of this astounding resource required the establishment of additional light stations. Most of these new lighthouses, which began to be built about 1910, were placed on or near the outer coast facing the open ocean.

The thing that makes Alaska special is its pristine wilderness environment. Lighthouses in Alaska are surrounded by some of the world's most spectacular scenery. Counting all its bays and fjords, Alaska has almost 34,000 miles of coastline, more than all of the rest of the United States combined. But historically, only a handful of lighthouses have marked the waters of Alaska.

Fishing boats ply the Inside Passage.

Alaska's fishing industry expanded rapidly during the early decades of the twentieth century, especially in the southeast where salmon canneries and herring processing plants sprang up on the outer islands. To keep the conveyor belts running, increasing numbers of fishing boats groped along the rocky outer coast or threaded foggy narrows to deliver their catch. To help fishermen reach their destinations safely, maritime authorities placed a light on Cape Decision at the southern end of Kuiu Island, about 60 miles south of Sitka, the old Russian capital.

Cape Decision earned its name by forcing mariners to choose between two key passages. Sumner Strait headed east toward Wrangell, while Chatham Strait went north toward the more populated areas of Juneau, Haines, and Skagway. Despite its importance, the cape was marked for many years by a small, untended acetylene light. Finally in 1932 it received a fully equipped lighthouse and fog signal station with resident keepers.

This light station had an all-business appearance when it was built, and it still does today. The 40-foot tower rises from the flat roof of a square, reinforced-concrete fog signal building. Originally the lantern room held a third-order Fresnel lens, but a Vega-style automated light has now replaced it.

The station had quarters for at least three resident keepers, but no one has lived here full-time since 1974, when the light was automated. Like other long-empty lighthouses, this one has declined during the many years since its Coast Guard keepers moved on to other duties. But it has found an important friend in Karen Johnson.

"I was inspired to adopt the Cape Decision Lighthouse because I love this land," says Johnson, who has lived in the area for more than twenty-five years. "I wanted to claim it for the local people, the villages that would benefit economically from whatever happened here."

To care for the light station and put it to use for the benefit of the local population, Johnson has formed a nonprofit organization called the Cape Decision Lighthouse Society. "The society is dedicated to the preservation of the lighthouse and surrounding wilderness areas," she says. "We would like to see them used for public recreation."

Among the society's short-term goals is repair of a large wooden dock that burned in 1989, but a complete restoration of the station is likely to take years. "At first I was overwhelmed by the enormity of the project," says Johnson. "We've worked through a lot of the difficulties, but we have a long row to hoe."

Established in 1932, the **Cape Decision Light** marks a turning point where mariners must choose between two key passages. Resident crews maintained the station until 1974 when the light was automated. Nowadays it is cared for by a nonprofit lighthouse society.

Johnson believes all the hard work is worthwhile, however. Cape Decision has special meaning for Johnson, and she believes others will share her appreciation of it. "I really enjoy the quiet and solitude when I come out to Cape Decision," she says. "There's a timelessness you experience out here."

Keeping Up the Keeper's Tradition

Time does not stand still, not even for lighthouses. Recent decades have radically changed the way lighthouses are perceived and how they are maintained. Once part of the workaday world of the commercial mariner, they are now looked upon more as historical monuments than as necessary signposts for navigators. The rugged coast of Alaska is among the few places where lighthouses remain vital to shipping. Even so, the lights are no longer cared for by full-time resident keepers.

Although Alaska's lighthouses remain important, if not essential, for safe navigation in the far north, the old sentinels now stand alone. But their automated beacons still require occasional maintenance and repair. The job of caring for the far-flung lights falls to special

Randy Keaveny

teams operating out of Coast Guard bases at Sitka, Ketchikan, and elsewhere. In most cases the all-but-inaccessible lights must be reached by helicopter.

"Doing Aides to Navigation work in Alaska is different," says Randy Keaveny, former officer in charge of the Coast Guard's 17th District Aides to Navigation Team. "Everything we fly to is remote, very remote. When you come to a lighthouse to work, you are not going to be picked up by a truck. You are not going to be picked up by a passing boat. You are going to get here by helicopter, and that is how you are going to leave."

Lighthouses in Alaska are serviced once every three months. The beacons are powered by batteries, which are kept charged by solar panels, so all the electrical systems must be thoroughly checked. "When we arrive at a lighthouse, we test the batteries for voltage to make sure the solar array is keeping them fully charged," says Keaveny. "Then we check the solar array to make sure none of the panels are cracked or broken. From there we move inside to work the lantern, the bulbs, or the lamps."

Perched on a barren rock about 70 miles west of Juneau, the **Cape Spencer Lighthouse** was always difficult to maintain and supply. Automated in 1974, its beacon continues to guide mariners, but without the assistance of full-time keepers.

Among the eleven Alaskan light stations regularly serviced by Coast Guard teams is the one at Cape Spencer. Perched like a giant seabird on a barren rock about 70 miles northwest of Juneau, the Cape Spencer Lighthouse was always considered exceptionally remote. Keepers here had to travel half a day or more to get mail, purchase supplies, or visit a physician.

Because of its isolation Cape Spencer was among the last of Alaska's key navigational turning points to receive a lighthouse. In 1913 a small, automated acetylene beacon was placed here to mark the strategic channel through Icy Strait, but construction of a full-function light station with light, fog signal, and a residence for keepers did not begin for another ten years. It cost the U.S. government more than $175,000 to build a lighthouse on this remote and rocky site, but by 1925 the station was complete. A compact, every-thing-in-one structure, it consisted of a square, 25-foot tower rising from the roof of a rein-forced-concrete fog signal building, which also served as a dwelling. While the Cape Spencer beacon remains operational, no one has lived here since 1974, when the light was automated. The station's original third-order Fresnel lens has been removed and replaced by a solar-powered Vega optic. The old Fresnel lens is now on display at the Alaska State Museum in Juneau.

Rebuilding an "Indestructible" Lighthouse

Also automated in 1974 was the Cape Hinchinbrook Lighthouse located near the entrance to Prince William Sound, one of the world's most scenic and economi-cally vital ocean inlets. A magnet for freighters, passenger liners, and fishing trawlers, the sound has served as a marine highway since Russian fur traders first visited its shores in the 1740s. Today it also serves as a thoroughfare for supertankers loaded with oil from the Alaska Pipeline.

Recognizing the importance of the sound, the Lighthouse Service established a major light station at Cape Hinchinbrook at the southwest end of Hinchinbrook Island. Com-pleted in 1909 at a cost of $125,000, it was at that time the most modern and best built lighthouse in the northwest. So solid were its walls and foundation that some described the station as "indestructible," but nature would soon prove this lighthouse even more vulner-able than most.

In 1927 and again in 1928, powerful earthquakes rocked the southern coast of Alaska, shearing huge slabs of rock from the Cape Hinchinbrook cliffs. Soon the teetering light-house stood so near the edge of the precipice that it had to be abandoned.

Construction of a new lighthouse for Cape Hinchinbrook was not undertaken until 1933. Lighthouse officials placed legendary builder Michael Harris in charge of the project.

The powerful **Cape Hinchinbrook** beacon outshines the full moon. Assigned the task of guiding mariners into the commercially vital, but environmentally sensitive, Prince William Sound, it is con-sidered Alaska's most important navigational light. The art deco—style tower shown here dates to 1935 when it replaced an earlier lighthouse that was weakened by earthquakes.

Elmer Harris lived at Cape Hinchinbrook during the 1930s while his father supervised construction of its lighthouse.

Harris erected most of the lighthouses that still stand in Alaska today. In part he was responsible for the art deco styling for which Alaska's light towers are known. At Hinchinbrook, Harris built yet another art deco structure. Completed in 1935, the reinforced-concrete tower and fog signal building stood on a foundation of stone well back from the cliff.

While working at Cape Hinchinbrook, Harris had with him his teenage son Elmer. "At that time my dad was superintendent of construction for the Department of Commerce Lighthouse Service," says Elmer Harris. "He had built practically all the lighthouses in Alaska and some in Washington State as well. I was with him at Cape Hinchinbrook during the summers of 1933 and 1934, and in 1935 when the lighthouse was finished."

A family crisis had left the elder Harris little option but to keep Elmer and his other children with him while he worked. "My mother had passed away when I was four, my brother Leif was six, and my brother Karl was eight. It was a rather traumatic death, so Captain Dabrell, who was head of the lighthouse district, called my dad and said he wouldn't be remiss at all if he wanted to take us to the stations with him."

As a result Elmer Harris and his brothers saw several of Alaska's lighthouses while they were under construction, including those at Tree Point, Mary Island, and Cape Hinchinbrook. "It was nice to grow up in an area where I was either hunting or fishing or doing something to help my father with his job."

At the Ends of the Earth

Among the lighthouses Michael Harris built in Alaska was an impressive five-story structure at Scotch Cap. Located on Unimak Island in the Aleutians, Scotch Cap was extraordinarily remote even when compared to other Alaska lighthouses. Beginning at the far southwestern corner of mainland Alaska, the Aleutian Islands stretch toward Asia in a rugged, 1,000-mile-long arch. Constantly under siege by high waves and howling winds blowing in off the frigid Bering Sea, the islands are mostly barren and so inhospitable that families were never allowed at Aleutian light stations.

Because of its smoking volcanic peaks, the Native American Aleuts called Unimak Island the "Roof of Hell." Many of the keepers and assistant keepers who served here likely thought that an apt description for the island. Forced to endure horrendous weather and isolation for a year or more at a time, Scotch Cap keepers had to be tough. Nature and circumstances left them no choice. Still, there were always men willing to live and work here at the outermost rim of the continent.

Some Alaska keepers, such as Ted Pederson, relished their lengthy stints in faraway outposts and even brought a certain gusto to them. Unlike Pederson, however, most of the

The first **Scotch Cap Lighthouse** was built in 1903 at the tip of Unimak Island to guide ships of the Alaska Gold Rush through the Aleutian Islands to Nome. Four decades later, the weathered old wooden lighthouse was replaced by a new structure built of durable concrete and steel. That lighthouse, pictured here, was destroyed by a tsunami in 1946.

The USCGC *Anthony Petit* is named for a lighthouse keeper killed at Scotch Cap in 1946. A keeper-class Coast Guard tender, the *Petit* services Alaskan light stations, buoys, and other navigational markers.

keepers at Scotch Cap were not the sort to hike hundreds of miles in winter just to meet a lady. Most had friends and loved ones waiting for them back home—whether that be in Anchorage, Miami, Rochester, New York, or Topeka—when their long stint in the Aleutians was over. And while at Scotch Cap, they had a very important job to do. Mariners relied on their beacon to guide them through Unimak Pass, which linked the Bering Sea to the Pacific. No doubt the light served an inspirational purpose as well. Mariners looked to Scotch Cap as a last lonely outpost of civilization, a last reminder of home before they passed into the dark void of the ocean.

An octagonal wooden lighthouse had marked Scotch Cap since 1903, but by 1940 it had been replaced by one of Harris's modern-looking art deco structures. The new lighthouse was rock solid, its concrete walls reinforced with iron rods. The tower held aloft a powerful third-order Fresnel lens, while the lower stories housed an equally muscular fog signal. Squeezed in among the clutter of generators, batteries, boilers, and other equipment were living quarters for five crewmen.

Chuck Jones, USCG

During the early months of 1946, those quarters were occupied by Anthony Petit, Jack Colvin, Paul Ness, Leonard Pickering, and Dewey Dykstra. Petit, a career coastguardsman, was the head keeper. One of the Coast Guard tenders that now services lighthouses in Alaska has been named for him.

"We're on board the USCGC *Anthony Petit*," says commanding officer Charles "Chuck" Jones. The *Petit* is a specialized vessel, one of the U.S. Coast Guard's keeper-class tenders, each of which is named for a lighthouse keeper. There is a plaque on board honoring chief boatswain mate Anthony Petit. "It was presented to us by the admiral during the commissioning of the ship," says Jones. "It's a replica of the plaque that's out at the site of the old lighthouse."

Both plaques serve as memorials and reminders of the tragic events that took place at Scotch Cap during the early hours of April 1, 1946. It was April Fools' Day, but the shaking that tumbled the Scotch Cap keepers out of bed at about 1:30 that morning was no joke. It was an undersea earthquake so powerful that it sucked the water from Unimak Pass, the broad channel in front of the lighthouse.

The station likely suffered minor damage from the quake. No doubt there were broken dishes, chunks of fallen plaster, and overturned supplies scattered about the floor, but the light remained in operation. The real disaster, however, struck about forty-five minutes after the quake, when the water that had drained from Unimak Pass returned—all at once.

No one will ever know whether the keepers could see it coming, the 100-foot-high tidal wave barreling towards them at 500 miles per hour. If they did see it, they had only a moment to prepare for what was about to happen. There was no escape.

Located far above Scotch Cap atop the Unimak Island cliffs was a small radio direction-finding station. Its crew survived the calamity and afterward hurried to see what the tidal wave had done to the Scotch Cap Lighthouse and the men stationed there. Nothing remained of the seemingly impregnable concrete-and-steel building but scattered chunks of rubble. The bodies of the five Scotch Cap keepers were later recovered as they washed up along the shore.

The lighthouse at Scotch Cap was never rebuilt. Today the task of guiding mariners safely through Unimak Pass is handled by an automated light shining from a skeleton tower perched on a ledge more than 100 feet above the sea. All that remains to mark the site of the original station is the plaque placed here in memory of Petit, Colvin, Ness, Pickering, and Dykstra. Like all worthy memorials, however, it honors not just those whose names are inscribed on it, but an entire class of brave men and women. In this case the honor belongs to all those who, for more than a century, have struggled to light the coasts of a still untamed Great Land.

Scattered wreckage is all that remained of **Scotch Cap** after a 100-foot tsunami stormed ashore in 1946. Five keepers including Anthony Petit were killed in the disaster. Today, mariners who brave Aleutian blizzards and wild seas are guided by a simple, unmanned light on a skeletal tower on Unimak Island.

EASTERN GREAT LAKES

Lighting America's Inland Waterway

Although inactive for nearly half a century, the **Rock Island Lighthouse** near Clayton, New York, is kept in presentable condition by local volunteers. Here it greets one of the countless freighters that follow the St. Lawrence Seaway to the heart of the continent.

Highway to the Heartland

"Lighthouses stand at the edge of things," says Mike Vogel. "And there has always been a magic in that boundary. They're a symbol of our desire to push outward but to always have that security of a way back home."

Vogel, an editorial writer for a newspaper in Buffalo, New York, is an expert on lighthouses and the role they have played in the growth and development of the American Midwest. Although located far inland, Buffalo is a seaport, a status it shares with dozens of other Great Lakes cities, all of them hundreds of miles from the Atlantic. The busiest inland waterway on the planet, the Great Lakes are accessible to oceangoing vessels by way of the St. Lawrence Seaway.

The lakes have long served as a liquid highway. During the early 1600s Europeans began to explore the Great Lakes region in search of the fabled Northwest Passage said by some to link the Atlantic and Pacific Oceans. They pushed hundreds of miles up the St. Lawrence River, beyond which they discovered what appeared to be a vast network of inland seas. But time and again, when the explorers lifted these waters to their lips, they could detect no salt. Instead of seas, these were *great lakes* with no ocean outlet except by way of the St. Lawrence.

As it turned out, the Northwest Passage existed only in the minds of early adventurers and mariners who had hoped to use it for trading voyages to China and Japan. The lakes were real enough, however, and eventually would prove far more valuable than any trade route to the Orient. Combined with the river, they provided a 1,500-mile watery thoroughfare straight to heart of a continent. Serving as a fast and inexpensive transportation system,

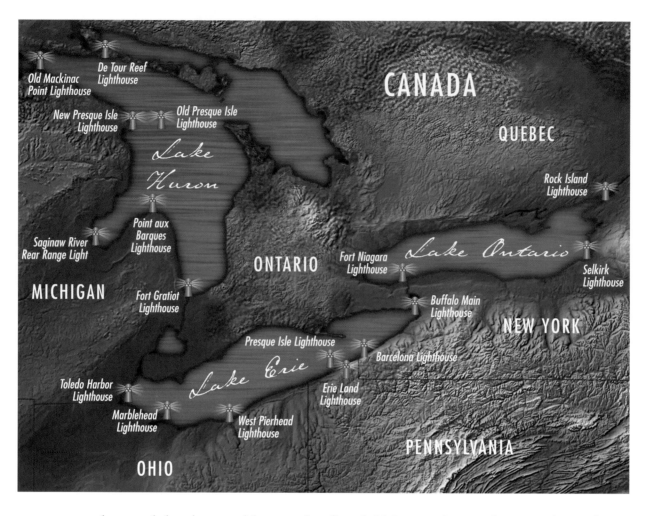

they speeded settlement of the agriculturally rich Midwest and in time became a driving force in the economies of two nations. But none of this would have been possible without the long chain of lighthouses that rose up along the lakes as the nations themselves grew strong.

Gateway to the Great Lakes

To reach the Great Lakes, Atlantic shipping must pass through the 500-mile-long corridor formed by the St. Lawrence River. For the last 100 miles or so of this distance, the river serves as the border between the United States and Canada. As it approaches Lake Ontario, the river narrows and its flow is broken by countless stony outcroppings, some several miles long and others mere scraps of rock. This is the famed Thousand Islands region where lake-bound freighters must negotiate a torturous maze of channels.

For more than a hundred years the Rock Island Lighthouse helped mariners pass safely through this labyrinth. Constructed in 1847 and rebuilt in 1882, it marked a small river island about 4 miles northeast of Clayton, New York, and a few miles southwest of the Thousand Islands Bridge. The 40-foot limestone tower still stands with its feet in the water just off the north side of the island. Countless mariners owe their safe passage through this dangerous stretch of river to the tower, which once held a sixth-order Fresnel lens. But the lens is gone now and so are the keepers who once lived here with their families in the station's rambling dwelling. Deactivated in 1958, the lighthouse is no longer used for navigation. To many of those who live nearby, however, it remains an important reminder of earlier times.

Rock Island Lighthouse

Manny Jerome has been visiting Rock Island for nearly sixty years. "I just think this is one of the world's better spots," says Jerome, who now helps keep the station presentable. "For the last twenty years, I've been kind of a self-appointed caretaker of this place. The St. Lawrence Seaway brings ships

Manny Jerome rows to his adopted lighthouse.

from many different countries and people from all over the world, so it's important that this lighthouse be dressed up and look nice."

Enormous seagoing vessels still pass close to the island. "We just take it for granted when they go by," says Jerome. "We don't pay that much attention, but some of these ships are 730 feet long. It's almost as if you could reach out and touch them."

Jerome's personal link to the lighthouse runs deep. "Back in the early 1950s, when I was a child, we'd watch the light," he says. "When the light came on, we knew it was time to go to bed."

A lifelong summer resident of nearby Wellesley Island, Jerome first worked at the light station when he was seven or eight years old. He and his brother would row across to Rock Island and volunteer their services to the U.S. Coast Guard keeper. "We would help him carry fuel for the generators," he says. "And we'd have fun. We swam, had picnics, and just generally enjoyed the place."

Jerome's fascination with the lighthouse was rekindled after the station was deactivated and its buildings began to fall into disrepair. "The lighthouse was in very bad condition," he says. "The exterior was falling away, the grounds were overgrown, and nobody was taking care of anything over here on the island."

Although still cared for by Manny Jerome and other helpful locals, the **Rock Island Lighthouse** is now part of a peaceful state park. The beacon is a stoic reminder of bygone days.

Eventually Jerome decided that something had to be done. The state of New York now owned the lighthouse, but had many other more urgent uses for its funds. So in 1983 Jerome collected contributions from his neighbors and, with permission from the state, began a privately funded effort to fix up the old light station. Mortar was replaced and patched, the exterior was painted, and the grounds cleaned up. A flagpole was acquired from the Winter Olympics site at Lake Placid, and a light was returned to the long empty lantern room. Although not useful to ships, the light gives Rock Island the appearance of a fully operational light station. Still cared for by Jerome, his family, and the New York State Department of Parks, Recreation and Historical Preservation, the lighthouse now serves as an attraction for summertime visitors.

"They don't build lighthouses anymore, so obviously this is a historical monument," Jerome says. "I felt it was being left for nature to destroy it and that it was time someone did something to preserve the history. It's a labor of love and something that's a big part of my life. I want to make sure that it's here for generations to come."

Salmon Fishermen's Light

About an hour south of the Thousand Islands Bridge, the Salmon River flows into Mexico Bay in the far southeastern corner of Lake Ontario. The glorious runs of Atlantic salmon that gave the river its name are gone, but there are still plenty of fish to be caught here. These waters have been restocked with Pacific salmon, to the delight of anglers who come here to hook these hard-fighting fish.

"The folks up in Alaska laugh at us and say we've got the small kings," says Jim Walker. "Well, the record here for a king salmon is forty-seven pounds and thirteen ounces. That's a pretty substantial fish in anybody's book."

Catches of impressive size are often made in the autumn near the small town of Pulaski, which nestles on the banks of the river. Some salmon are hooked within site of the historic Selkirk Lighthouse located down near the river mouth. Built in 1838, the stone lighthouse has become almost a part of the landscape. Decommissioned only twenty years after it was placed in operation, the old government building has been in private hands for nearly one and a half centuries. Now owned by Walker, it is used as an inn for anglers.

An avid angler himself, Walker came here from Maine on a sportfishing expedition during the 1980s. Having fallen in love with the area and its runs of salmon, he decided to stay. Walker opened a tackle shop and, almost as an afterthought, bought the Selkirk Lighthouse. In time he grew fascinated with the rustic structure.

Salmon River catches can be impressive.

Jim Walker

"As it turned out, it became the focal point of everything we do," Walker says.

The Selkirk Lighthouse is, in fact, a historic treasure. Because it was deactivated at an early date—1858—and never rebuilt or refitted by the Lighthouse Service, it retains many unusual architectural features. Outstanding among them is the birdcage lantern at the top of the tower.

"We have one of only four remaining birdcage lanterns in North America," says Walker, who is determined to preserve the structure's unique features. "This early style of

lantern featured small panes of glass. But unfortunately this design interfered with the beacon and made it difficult to see the light from any kind of distance offshore."

The Selkirk birdcage lantern was the work of the famed—some would say notorious—lighthouse contractor and former sea captain Winslow Lewis. Although not a trained engineer, Lewis was a crafty businessman who used his Treasury Department connections to win contracts for the design and construction of one government lighthouse after another. Many of these structures proved decidedly poor in quality. Equally questionable were the various lighthouse lamps, reflectors, and lenses Lewis claimed to have invented—some were rough copies of English devices. The Selkirk birdcage housed one of his more dubious designs—a bottle-green glass magnifying lens intended to broaden the lamp's visibility. But the crude lens only made a bad light worse, mariners said.

The unique birdcage-style lantern room at the Selkirk Lighthouse was handcrafted by a local blacksmith more than 160 years ago.

Although out of service for more than a century, the Selkirk Light is shining once again. Most likely its beacon is much stronger than in Lewis' day. Having received permission from the Coast Guard to operate the light as a private aide to navigation, Walker has placed a small modern optic in the original Lewis birdcage. To pay for this and other maintenance costs, Walker rents the lighthouse to overnight guests, many of them fishermen.

"Fishermen tend to come here for one reason only and that's to fish," Walker says. "I'd like to think we're also giving them encouragement to learn about this lighthouse."

Fortress Light of the Niagara

Cutting across a 30-mile-wide neck of limestone in western New York, the Niagara River connects Lake Ontario with Lake Erie. Tumbling over American and Horseshoe Falls, the river creates one of the most majestic natural wonders on the planet. But the falls are much more than a grand spectacle and magnet for tourists and newlyweds. They are also a giant obstacle to the flow of shipping and commerce in the lower Great Lakes.

Built in 1838, the fieldstone **Selkirk Lighthouse** is now privately owned. Despite its rustic appearance, it provides comfortable accommodations for anglers attracted by annual salmon runs in the nearby river and others looking for a unique getaway.

The **Fort Niagara Lighthouse** once marked the mouth of the Niagara River, one of the few natural harbors on the western end of Lake Ontario. Because it was the easiest portage around Niagara Falls, most commercial traffic passed through this port. Before the opening of the Erie Canal in 1825 this lighthouse marked one of the busiest and most important places on the Great Lakes.

"Niagara Falls formed the ultimate speed bump," says historian Brian Dunnigan, an expert on the maritime history of the eastern Great Lakes. "Early travelers were clearly impressed by the majesty of the falls. But they did require a portage of about 6 miles."

Westbound passengers and goods had to be off-loaded at Niagara and shunted around the falls to the nearest safely navigable stretch of the river. To reach the most popular portage route, vessels on Lake Ontario would make for the mouth of the Niagara not far downriver from the roaring falls.

"During the day a mariner sailing across Lake Ontario could find the Niagara by watching for the great plume of vapor rising from the falls," says Dunnigan. "But at night it was all too easy to sail past the mouth of the river."

To mark the portage and protect this strategic place, the French built a fort in 1726. They are also said to have put in place a modest light to guide ships. Having captured the fort during the French and Indian War, the British established a more substantial navigational light here in 1780.

"The light was constructed on top of a large domed building, which today is generally called the French Castle," says Dunnigan. "Actually the castle was the officers quarters at Fort Niagara."

Following the Revolutionary War U.S. forces took control of the fort and its light. "The U.S. Army officers who lived here complained about the lighthouse and about the keeper tromping through the building carrying highly flammable lamp oil," says Dunnigan. "As a result a new site just to the south of the fort was selected for a more modern light. By 1872 Fort Niagara's new light was functioning."

The "French Castle" officers quarters at Fort Niagara

Shining from the top of a 52-foot octagonal stone tower, the new Fort Niagara Lighthouse would serve mariners for more than 120 years. Deactivated in 1993, it is now a tourist attraction that is part of Old Fort Niagara. The station's service building houses a gift shop and museum.

Even with a fine light to attract ships, Niagara was not destined to become a major port. Mariners and the commercial interests they represented were dissatisfied with the costs and delays caused by the portage, and they sought a more convenient route around the falls. By 1825 they had one—the Erie Canal.

A Canal, a City, and a Lighthouse

As the Niagara harbor and portage declined, other transportation centers deeper into the Great Lakes region rose in importance. Prominent among these was Buffalo, the western terminus of the Erie Canal. Located at the eastern end of Lake Erie, Buffalo attracted commerce from all the lakes and, hence, from the entire Midwest.

Even before the opening of the canal, U.S. government officials had recognized the strategic importance of Buffalo. So, too, did the British, who burned the city during the War of 1812. But Buffalo quickly recovered from this blow, and by 1818 a major lighthouse marked its bustling harbor. With the opening of the canal, the city burgeoned.

Still a bustling commercial hub, Buffalo, New York, was once the gateway to the west. Strategically positioned between Lakes Ontario and Erie, it ranked among the busiest ports in the world but eventually lost much of its lake trade to the railroads.

"The single most important event in the history of Buffalo was the opening of the Erie Canal," says Mike Vogel. "Within a decade the city's population had quadrupled. By the end of the nineteenth century, Buffalo was the eighth largest city in the country and the seventh busiest port in the world."

The original lighthouse soon proved inadequate to its task, and in 1833 a new stone tower was built at the end of a 1,400-foot pier. An octagonal limestone structure rising 68 feet above the lake, the old tower still stands.

"We think it's a pretty lighthouse," says Vogel. "We think it's one of the prettiest on the lakes."

A career journalist, Vogel devotes spare time to the Buffalo Lighthouse Association, an organization dedicated to the preservation of the Buffalo Main Lighthouse and other historic structures in the area. "Some people may wonder why a newspaperman would get involved with lighthouses," he says. "Well, when you think about it, they're not that different. Newspapers are lighthouses in the world of ideas. Same job, different setting."

This historical light overlooks the terminus of the Lake Erie Canal. Now a cherished monument to Buffalo's maritime past, the 1833 **Buffalo Main Lighthouse** guided countless lake freighters to the city's wharves. Deactivated in 1914, the old lighthouse was handsomely refurbished and relit during the 1990s.

Journalist and historian Mike Vogel at work

Buffalo Main Lighthouse

In the eyes of many, the Buffalo Main beacon is more than just a navigational light. The venerable tower serves as a symbol for the city itself. "This tower was old when the Statue of Liberty was erected in New York Harbor [1886]," says Vogel. "It was older still when Ellis Island opened." (The famed receiving station on Ellis Island began processing immigrants in 1892.)

Much like New York City, Buffalo became a funnel for people on the move. Uncounted thousands of settlers used the city and its harbor as their gateway to the rich lands of the American heartland. "That river of humanity sailed out past this lighthouse," Vogel says.

From the middle of the nineteenth century onward, westward immigration across the lakes was aided by the latest lighthouse technology. In 1857 the lantern room at the top of the tower was fitted with a powerful third-order Fresnel lens. Invented and produced by the French, Fresnel lenses were far superior to other lighthouse optics in use at the time.

"In the early 1800s lighthouse engineers didn't have a whole lot to work with in terms of illumination," says Vogel. "They worked with oil lamps that had maybe seven or eight candlepower, so they needed a very powerful lens or reflector system to magnify the light and use every bit of it. Eventually the French came up with the Fresnel lens, a structure of bronze, brass, and glass that captures light and concentrates it into a tight beam that can be used by mariners."

With this new technology to guide vessels, Buffalo's harbor grew even busier, but its glory days could not last forever. Like the harbor at Fort Niagara, it eventually fell into decline. Railroads cut deeply into the commercial traffic that once flowed so freely along the Erie Canal and through Buffalo. Eventually Canada's Welland Canal, just west of the Niagara River, would bypass Buffalo all together.

"There's not much left from that earlier era of growth, prosperity, and expansion," Vogel says. "But the lighthouse will always be here. The single, steady, unchanging presence of that whole scene, the sentinel that has stood front and center, is the lighthouse. It's a landmark of the American Journey."

Gas Light at Barcelona

Some landmarks of America's westward expansion are all but forgotten. Among the more unusual of these is a lighthouse located in the village of Barcelona, New York, about an hour's drive by interstate to the west of Buffalo. Buffalo was not the only community to benefit from the opening of the Erie Canal and the accompanying surge of westbound settlers and commerce. The citizens of tiny Barcelona located so nearby to Lake Erie saw great things in store for their town. Such was their confidence that they convinced the government to build a lighthouse—even though their harbor was at the time a little-used backwater.

A modest conical tower constructed of boulders and stones gathered from nearby fields, this lighthouse was not much to look at, but it had one distinction. Its lamps were among the first anywhere to burn natural gas. Not far from the tower was an extraordinary pool of

Now a private residence, the fieldstone **Barcelona Lighthouse** dates to 1829. Although active for only thirty years, the station can claim a curious historic distinction—its beacon was once powered by natural gas piped in from a nearby well.

The lantern room that enclosed Barcelona's gas-powered beacon was removed more than a century ago. The structure seen atop the old stone tower nowadays is for show only.

water that had been known to catch fire. Enterprising residents placed a masonry cap on this burning spring and piped the gas to the lighthouse.

In time the well ran out of gas and so, too, did the dreams of locals who hoped their little town would become the next Buffalo. The well produced only sporadic puffs after 1838, and the lighthouse keeper was forced to install oil lamps. In 1859 the light itself was discontinued, and the tower and residence sold to private owners.

The 40-foot fieldstone tower still stands. Although of little use to ships or the sleepy little lakeside community it once served, the tower remains as a monument to American workmanship and American aspirations.

A Dream Home in Erie

The American Dream takes many forms. For Patrick and Mary Scutella, the dream was to live in a lighthouse—and now they do. Every so often Erie, Pennsylvania, holds a lottery to see who will get to live in the stone lighthouse overlooking the town and the lake. The Scutellas were delighted when they won.

"How many people get to live at a historic site?" asks Mary Scutella. "Not too many. And so we count ourselves very lucky."

The lighthouse is very historic, indeed, and so is the town of Erie. Originally Pennsylvania had no direct access to the Great Lakes, but in 1792 the commonwealth bought a 45-mile stretch of the Lake Erie shoreline. Included in the purchase was a fine harbor at what is now the port of Erie. Protected from the stormy waters of the lake by a long, arching peninsula, the harbor was a sizable one, and it would prove a useful asset for both the commonwealth of Pennsylvania and the U.S. military. It was here that, during the War of 1812, Commodore Oliver Hazard Perry built the warships with which he defeated the British Great Lakes fleet. Without that victory the British colony of Canada might have snatched away much of the Great Lakes region.

Erie's harbor would also attract plenty of commercial traffic, and in time the city would have three lighthouses. Near the end of the North Pier, a square, wrought-iron tower with tapered walls marks the entrance to the harbor. Dating to 1927, it replaced a wooden tower that was knocked over by a ship.

No such accident was ever likely to damage the Erie Land Lighthouse, for it is located well away from the harbor on a hill in the town. Built in 1867, it took the place of a half-century-old stone tower that had begun to lean dangerously out of plumb and threatened to topple over. The replacement served well for better than thirty years, but its light was finally deactivated in 1900. Although it has been out of service for more than a century, the Erie Land Lighthouse still stands, and it is here that the Scutellas now make their home.

Patrick and Mary Scutella

The Erie Land Lighthouse, located near Erie, Pennsylvania

The privilege of living at the lighthouse carries with it considerable responsibility. "When we first moved in, we very much got the impression that we were supposed to just caretake the place for the city," says Patrick Scutella. "We were to shut the gate and just make sure the place was maintained."

As it turned out, however, the Scutellas have thrown the gates wide open for visitors. The Erie Land Lighthouse is now a very popular city attraction. Says Mary Scutella: "Pat and I made a pact between ourselves when we first moved in that if we got tired of people coming onto the property, then we were the wrong people for this place. History needs to be shared, and the only way to do that is to be open about it."

The way Patrick Scutella sees it, history is about people and the lighthouse belongs to the people of Erie. "We're a very ethnic, blue collar, hard-working town," he says. "I've seen pictures of people who spent time down here at the lighthouse when they were children. Some of our elderly people and their kids grew up in this neighborhood, and the lighthouse is a symbol to them."

The lighthouse still attracts plenty of children. "It's good to see the children playing near the lighthouse," says Scutella. "When children enjoy reveling in her shadow, the history sort of takes hold. Maybe in a quiet, subtle way, the lighthouse itself is a history lesson, and it is still teaching that lesson today."

Almost an Island

While the Land Light welcomed ships to the city's harbor, Erie's third lighthouse warned them away from the constantly shifting sands of the peninsula that had created it. The first light station at that spot was established in 1819, but the lighthouse was rebuilt in 1867 and again in 1873. Now more than one and a quarter centuries old, the existing Presque Isle Lighthouse is still guiding mariners.

"The words Presque Isle mean 'almost an island'," says Loretta Brandon. The peninsula is, in fact, almost an island. "Its 3,200 acres of land are connected by a very narrow neck to the city of Erie. There have been times during severe storms when water has washed over the neck and made Presque Isle into a real island. A lot of people got stranded when that happened."

Brandon is the daughter of one of Presque Isle's caretakers, and for several years during

Pennsylvania's Presque Isle Lighthouse

Loretta Brandon

her childhood, the light station was home. "I lived in the Presque Isle Lighthouse from 1956 until 1963," she says. "I was six years old when we moved here, and I didn't know that just by living here I was becoming part of the history of this place."

The history she remembers has a very personal ring to it, however. Presque Isle stands out in her memory as a place of peace, filled with the dreams and pleasures of childhood.

"My dad brought a lot of pets home," she says. "We had three Chesapeake Bay retrievers who were like siblings to me. They would hunt for my dad, but the one they loved best was the woman with the smell of dog chow on her hands. And, of course, that was my mother."

The family also had a pet raccoon named Inky. "Inky grew to be a very important part of the family," says Brandon. "But he wreaked a lot of havoc in the house."

Having made a meal of yet another family pet— a small turtle—Inky may have suspected he had worn out his welcome. Soon afterwards he slipped back into the wilds.

Pennsylvania's two lighthouses are only a few miles apart, but the settings and stories behind both lights are very different. Located on a 7-mile finger of sand that stretches into Lake Erie, **Presque Isle** can still be a desolate place. In winter, the keepers of this lighthouse were the only residents for miles.

Brandon would also leave eventually, when her father moved on to another assignment, but she has held onto her fond memories of Presque Isle. "I wish I could come back again and live next to the lake," she says. "I wish I could hear the waves breaking as I'm going to sleep and have the peacefulness of a life close to nature."

Safe Harbors on a Deadly Lake

Nature is not just peace and quiet. It can have a very threatening side—as anyone who has ever been caught in one of Lake Erie's terrifying storms can testify. With an average depth of only 62 feet, Erie is the shallowest of the Great Lakes. This also makes it the most dangerous. Some early French voyagers referred to it as *Lac de Chaudière* or "the Boiler."

Tiny by comparison to the modern commercial towers in downtown Cleveland, the **West Pierhead Light** has warned vessels away from the city's west breakwater since 1911.

"Because the lake is so shallow, you have waves that are short and steep," says Mike Vogel. "They come hard, they come close together, and they can beat a vessel to pieces."

The lake's narrow width—only about 50 miles—is also a threat, especially to vessels caught in a storm. After all, a mariner fears the shore, with its ship-killing rocks and shallows, far more than the turbulence of open waters.

"On the ocean, you can ride out a storm," says Vogel. "But here you are never really that far from shore. You run out of room in a hurry. Once a ship's master loses control of his vessel, it will find the shore fairly quickly."

For almost a century the light towers marking Ohio's two biggest ports have guided imperiled ships to safety. These lighthouses are themselves like stout ships. The Toledo Harbor Light, for example, is as sturdy as they come. Perched atop a massive 12-foot-high platform of rock and concrete, it is built to withstand the lake's fury. Built in 1904, it is also an architectural wonder. Officially described as Romanesque, the stone-and-concrete structure seems part Victorian palace and part Russian Orthodox church. Nonetheless, it is a hardworking—one might even call it a blue-collar—light, which has guided many thousands of vessels to the safety of Toledo Harbor.

Somewhat less fanciful are the iron beacons that mark the east and west rims of the Cleveland Harbor entrance. Located near the end of a 3½-mile-long breakwater, the West

The **Toledo Harbor Lighthouse**, first lit in 1904, is about 8 miles off the Ohio shoreline. When the lighthouse was automated in 1966, the Coast Guard placed a mannequin dressed in a Coast Guard uniform in the window as a way of discouraging vandalism. In addition to its security duties, this unusual sentry created yet another lighthouse ghost story.

Pierhead Light dates to 1911. The spark-plug style cylinder of brick and cast iron has weathered countless storms. To help mariners reach port even in the heaviest weather, the station included a powerful foghorn. Its deep-throated call long ago earned it the nickname "cow." A few hundred yards away, the East Pierhead Light guards the other side of the entrance. Erected in 1910, it is only about half the size of its slightly younger sister across the harbor.

Neither of the existing Cleveland lights is as impressive as the grand navigational edifice that once served this city. Built in 1872, the high Victorian Cleveland Lighthouse stood on a hill overlooking the harbor and the city. Its huge, steep-roofed dwelling contained two separate residences and nearly twenty rooms. The main building and attached 87-foot brick tower were covered with ornate detailing. Although it remained in service for only about twenty years and was eventually demolished, it is remembered as one of America's most remarkable light stations.

Thunder on Lake Erie

While the Great Lakes have served the practical needs of westbound settlers and commercial interests for efficient transportation, they have also dazzled people with their extraordinary beauty. Generations of sightseers and vacationers have flocked to the lakes simply to enjoy themselves. To this day a favorite destination for outings is Lake Erie's South Bass Island, about 70 miles west of Cleveland and a few miles north of Sandusky. Since the 1850s people have been coming here just to have fun.

South Bass Island Lighthouse

The island also has served the needs of business. Completed in 1897, the South Bass Island Lighthouse helped guide an early twentieth-century boom of freighter traffic through Lake Erie's strategic South Passage. No longer active, the handsome brick structure is now owned by Ohio State University and used as a research facility.

There was no lighthouse on the island when Commodore Oliver Hazard Perry brought his small, wooden-hulled battle fleet to Put-in-Bay on the north side of South Bass Island. Vessels have often taken shelter from the weather in the protected waters of the bay, but that was not the commodore's purpose. He intended to stir up a storm on the lake, and that's exactly what he did.

When the War of 1812 broke out, the United States and Britain knew there was unfinished business between them and that it would now be settled. "The American Revolution ended in 1783," says Brian Dunnigan, historian and map curator at the Williams L. Clements Library. "But it ended with the British still controlling most of the forts on the Great Lakes."

The prospects for an American victory in another war were not good. "The British Navy was the largest and most powerful in the world at that time," says Dunnigan. "The U.S. Navy, although good, was very small. But tensions between the United States and Britain reached the boiling point in 1812, and Congress declared war."

Brian Dunnigan

The British were not just powerful at sea. They also maintained a substantial fleet on the Great Lakes. Unless it was defeated, the United States would likely lose control of the entire lakes region, and with it much of the Midwest. U.S. military officials placed the unenviable task of confronting the British fleet in the hands of Perry, a young and little known naval officer. There was no American fleet on the lakes, but Perry's men managed to build a few modest warships at Erie. Perry waited for the right opportunity. It came on September 10, 1813, when Perry met the British just to the west of Put-in-Bay, in one of the most important naval battles in American history.

An artist's conception of Perry's decisive victory at the Battle of Lake Erie, depicts American vessels taking advantage of their heavier cannon power as they close with the British.

In another archival print, Perry abandons his stricken flagship, the *Lawrence*. Soon he will board the *Niagara*, which remains in fighting trim, and lead his fleet to victory.

"Perry's vessels were armed with extremely powerful but very short-ranged weapons known as carronades," Dunnigan says. "The British had longer-range cannon, so it was critical for Perry to get into close quarters."

It is said the raging cannon duel could be heard all the way to Cleveland, as much as 70 to 80 miles to the east. Some on shore thought they were hearing thunder from a late summer storm breaking over the lake.

"Perry's flagship, the *Lawrence*, was badly damaged, and many of its crew killed or wounded," Dunnigan says. "Perry decided that his only hope was to transfer to his other large brig, the *Niagara*, and continue the attack from there."

Taking down his "Don't Give Up the Ship" flag, Perry abandoned the stricken *Lawrence* and rowed across to the *Niagara* in a small boat. Once on board, he rallied the American fleet. Perry ordered his hawkeyed riflemen into the rigging, from which they were able to clear the decks of the enemy ships. Soon the British were forced to surrender, and Perry was able to dispatch his famous, though sparsely worded, message: "We have met the enemy, and they are ours; two ships, two brigs, one schooner, and one sloop."

"In one afternoon the British lost control of Lake Erie and with it the upper Great Lakes," says Dunnigan. "Perry's victory was stunning. An entire British squadron had fallen to an American squadron."

A 352-foot granite column on South Bass Island now commemorates the battle and Oliver Hazard Perry's victory. The remains of both American and British officers killed in the battle are buried beneath the column, which serves as an international peace memorial. So tall and distinctive is the memorial that passing ships use it as a daymark or a daytime reference point.

Grandfather Light at Marblehead

On the mainland, several miles from South Bass Island, is a war/peace memorial of a very different sort. Johnson Island, just off Marblehead, Ohio, was used as a prisoner-of-war camp for Confederate officers during the Civil War. From the camp the Southerners could easily see the beacon of Marblehead Lighthouse, and it may have seemed to them that the lovely, flashing light was calling them to Dixie. Although many of the 10,000 Johnson Island prisoners died before the end of the war, most eventually made it back home. No doubt they took with them aching memories of the light. Some say they also took with them the sport of baseball, which at that time was not widely known in the South.

The Marblehead Lighthouse still shines today, more than 180 years after the station was established to guide vessels into Sandusky Bay. The oldest still-active lighthouse on the Great Lakes, it is now part of an Ohio state park. Each summer Mills Brandes tells visitors about the part he and his family played in the light's history.

"I used to live here with my grandfather, Mr. Charles A. Hunter," says Brandes. "He came here in 1903 and served as keeper of the Marblehead Lighthouse for thirty years.

"His first concern was that this is a very dangerous place to navigate. You have a rocky shore here with many reefs and very strong currents, so the light had to operate properly at all times. Mr. Hunter would stand watch—watching the light to make sure it was working and watching the lake to make sure there were no ships out there in trouble."

Karin Messner and Ro Chapman in character as Benajah and Rachel Wolcott

Charles Hunter had the longest tenure of any keeper in the history of Marblehead Lighthouse. He was also the station's second-to-last keeper. After he retired in 1933, the light was automated.

Just down the road from the tower, the memory of Marblehead's first keeper is being kept alive. Inside the original 1822 keeper's cottage, Ro Chapman and Karin Messner offer a living history demonstration for park visitors. Their performances are based on real events taken from the lives of the cottage's first residents. Chapman plays Benajah Wolcott, first

Keeper's cottage, Marblehead Lighthouse

Among the loveliest and most historic light towers on the Great Lakes, the **Marblehead Lighthouse** east of Port Clinton, Ohio, is a popular destination for tourists. This is also the oldest active lighthouse on the Great Lakes.

keeper of the Marblehead Lighthouse, and Messner plays Rachael Wolcott, the keeper's second wife.

Marblehead Lighthouse became a central aspect of their lives together. "Rachel probably did love this place as much as he did," Messner says. "This house," Chapman adds, "was built for Rachel by Benajah, as a wedding present."

Some parts of the drama are by no means lighthearted. "It was the year 1832 and there was a cholera epidemic," says Messner. "In those days, when people contracted cholera, there was no cure, so they were put on boats. When they died, the bodies were just thrown overboard. The bodies began washing up on the shore by the lighthouse. Benajah came to Rachael one day and said he couldn't stand seeing this any longer. He was going to give them a Christian burial. After touching the bodies, he contacted cholera himself and died."

After the tragic death of her husband, the government named Rachael Wolcott keeper of Marblehead Light. "Rachael was the first woman lighthouse keeper on the Great Lakes," says Messner. "She had to be very strong because the job was lonely and very demanding. Carrying whale oil up those steps was no small matter, and I believe she did it three times a day. Her children were quite young at the time."

Like the many visitors who come to Marblehead to take pictures, Chapman and Messner appreciate the beauty of the old lighthouse. But they are convinced that its history is even more valuable than its photogenic appearance. "It is beautiful," says Chapman. "It is probably the most frequently photographed place in the state of Ohio. But you also have to realize that there were many lonely hardworking souls who kept lights like this one burning."

Marblehead Lighthouse

A Green Light for Lake Freighters

North of Detroit, the St. Clair River forms the border between the United States and Canada. The river is also the link between Lake Erie and Lake Huron. More ships pass through here than through the Suez and Panama Canals combined. The Canadian Coast Guard is responsible for guiding maritime traffic through the narrow passage. Using an array of sophisticated electronic equipment not unlike that of an air-traffic control tower, they keep freighters almost as long as three football fields safely within their designated shipping lanes. But before the era of high technology, the hard work of guiding ships was shouldered by lighthouses.

In Port Huron on the Michigan side of the St. Clair stands the Fort Gratiot Lighthouse. The tower is older than the state itself.

"This lighthouse was 170 years old on November 1, 2000," says Bob Hanford. "We held a birthday party for it."

A member of the U.S. Coast Guard Auxiliary, Hanford is determined that the old lighthouse not be forgotten. As he sees it, the light still has a vital

Bob Hanford

function to perform. "The big ships now say they don't really use the light that much," he says. "But electronic equipment will fail, and if you don't have the light to guide you, then what are you going to do?"

The Fort Gratiot Light still beams out over Lake Huron. At night it's a welcome sight to pilots of the many smaller vessels that lack the latest electronic navigational gear. And it's always there just in case the big ships need it.

"The light can be seen from 18 miles out in the lake," says Hanford. "That is on a clear and normal evening, but, of course, we don't have too many of those around here."

Nowadays the lighthouse is popular, not just with mariners, but with the general public as well. Hanford offers tours of the station. "Year before last I had 5,002 people go through here," he says. "I guess they appreciate the fact that here's a structure that was built 170 years ago, and it's still standing."

The considerable age of its tower is not the only thing unusual about the Fort Gratiot Lighthouse. Its beacon is one of only a few that shine neither white nor red. The light is green.

About half a century ago, the clutter of powerful lights in a nearby rail yard had begun to confuse the pilots of vessels approaching Fort Gratiot. "The headlights of the locomotives were almost the same intensity

Bob Hanford stands in front of the **Fort Gratiot Lighthouse** where he serves as a U.S. Coast Guard Auxiliary keeper. He has guided thousands of visitors through the 170-year-old station.

as the light up in the tower," Hanford says. "This was confusing to ships, so lighthouse officials said, 'We'll just change that to green.' It has been green ever since."

Hanford points this out to visitors. When possible, he also takes them to the lantern room and gallery at the top of the 86-foot tower, from which they can enjoy a panoramic view of the lake and the river. Children are especially delighted by the experience.

"I only manage to make four trips up and down this thing each day," says Hanford. "I wish I could do more and accommodate more people, but those ninety-four steps are getting to my knees a bit. People just keep coming and coming, and I just keep plugging away. I go home at night and soak. I have a few spirits just to get joints working, and then I'm back the next day."

Despite the physical strain—a problem he shares with keepers of old—Hanford enjoys helping others celebrate the Fort Gratiot Light and its remarkable history. "I love it," he says. "I love working here."

Boat passing in front of the Fort Gratiot Lighthouse.

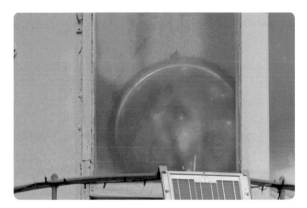

Fort Gratiot's unusual green beacon

Light on the Michigan Thumb

The Lower Michigan Peninsula is shaped lake a mitten with a rather fat thumb. Located on the eastern side of the peninsula, the thumb points resolutely northward, and a historic lighthouse marks its northernmost shore. The light station is called Point aux Barques, French for "Point of Little Boats." The name is a reference to the canoes of French fur traders who once frequented this place.

Nowadays Point aux Barques Lighthouse helps 1,000-foot-long freighters navigate safely around the point and into Saginaw Bay. The station's 89-foot brick tower dates to 1857, when it replaced an unsatisfactory stone lighthouse that had lasted only about ten years. Originally

a fourth-order Fresnel lens focused the light, but it was removed when the station was automated. Today the lighthouse employs a modern optic producing a whopping million candlepower beacon, the most powerful on the Great Lakes.

The Point aux Barques Light can be seen from up to 18 miles out in the lake. About that same distance to the west, another equally important navigational aide warns mariners away from a treacherous shoal. Built in open water more than a mile offshore, the Port Austin Reef Light has kept watch over the shoal since 1876.

"The Michigan thumb is the turning point for ships traveling into Saginaw Bay," says Lou Schillinger, who heads up the Port Austin Reef Light Preservation Society. "At the turn of the twentieth century, this was a very busy place, with over 300 ships per day passing the Port Austin Reef Lighthouse."

Port Austin Reef Lighthouse

Even with the lights in place to guide them, mariners often encountered trouble. "There are over 150 wrecked ships lying just off the Michigan thumb," says Schillinger. "They are strewn all along the channel—steam barges, sail barges, schooners, propeller-driven, iron-hulled freighters. They represent a kind of history book of shipping on the Great Lakes."

On Lake Huron, just as on the other lakes, weather is always a threat. With approximately 150 miles of open water between the Michigan thumb and the Canadian shore to the northeast, some storms can generate huge waves. "The storms of the Great Lakes usually come on very quickly, and they can be quite severe," Schillinger says.

Lou Schillinger

The worst storms come late in the year, especially in November. Every experienced Great Lakes sailor recognizes the threat represented by these late-season storms, but in the past financial pressures often forced captains to risk their vessels. "Shifting cargo could cause ships to take on water and sink," Schillinger says. "Waves oftentimes picked a freighter up at the stern and the bow, folding it in the middle. Many of these ships took a nosedive."

Perhaps the worst storm ever to strike the lakes swept into the Midwest during the first week of November 1913. The storm was the result of three huge weather systems—one each from the Gulf, the Pacific, and the Bering Sea—slamming into one another over the lakes.

Point aux Barques Lighthouse near Port Austin, Michigan, was first built in 1848 for $5,000. When it was rebuilt in 1857, it became the tallest and most powerful light on the Great Lakes. Today its impressive 89-foot brick tower has a 1-million candlepower beacon that shines 18 miles out into Lake Huron.

A FESTIVAL OF LIGHTS

Each October lighthouse lovers from all over the Great Lakes and around the world gather in the small town of Alpena on the northeastern shore of Michigan's Lower Peninsula. They come here to take part in the annual Great Lakes Lighthouse Festival, a four-day celebration of the region's maritime history. In recent years the event has attracted more than 40,000 visitors.

Michigan's New Presque Isle Light

"We get more and more people every year," says festival organizer Marv Theut. "Apparently there are a lot of people out there interested in lighthouses."

Festival activities typically include visits to nearby lighthouses such as the Old and New Presque Isle Lights about 20 miles north. Visitors are also treated to a series of lectures and talks by lighthouse veterans, authors, and experts. But the highlight of the festival is invariably the large lighthouse market at the Alpena Civic and Convention Center. Usually more than a hundred vendors are on hand to sell books, photographs, artwork, and artifacts, all related to lighthouses and maritime history. Among the offerings are, of course, more than a few model lighthouses—some small enough to fit onto a key chain and others too large to fit into an automobile. A few even have working beacons.

Old Presque Isle Light

"People have a lot of fun," says Theut. "They meet up with old friends and make new ones. But mostly they learn about an important part of our history that once was in danger of being forgotten altogether."

The festival raises money to help preserve some key reminders of the Great Lakes' maritime history. Abandoned light stations such as the one at Middle Island near Alpena are being restored with the help of festival funding.

"We're proud of what we've accomplished," Theut says. "We hope we can do more in the future."

Striking with little or no warning and extraordinary violence, the storm overtook dozens of large freighters far out on the lakes. The blizzard howled for five long days, and by the time its winds finally died down, nineteen ships lay wrecked.

Lake Huron was hit especially hard, and the storm showed no mercy to the vessels it caught there. One of these was the massive steamer *Howard M. Hanna.* She had tried to make a run for the shelter of Saginaw Bay, but she never made it.

"The *Hanna* was probably the most famous wreck in this particular area," says Schillinger. "At the height of the storm, the crew lost control of the *Hanna* and hit Port Austin Reef broadside."

The *Hanna* wrecked in the middle of the night. Blinded by the driving snow and sleet and the near total darkness, the Port Austin Reef keepers were at first unaware there had been a wreck near the lighthouse. But in the morning, they spotted the *Hanna's* broken hulk. All thirty-three of those on board the *Hanna* were rescued. They were the lucky ones, for elsewhere on the lakes, the great November storm of 1913 would claim 248 lives.

Saving Saginaw's Centennial Light

The protected waters that might have saved the *Hanna* made the Saginaw Bay a heavily trafficked thoroughfare for commercial shipping, especially during the late nineteenth and early twentieth centuries. At that time business was booming on the Great Lakes, and Bay City, located at the head of the bay, was a very busy port and shipbuilding center.

The area can boast a rich maritime history. "It's hard to be in Bay City if you are not into nautical history," says Ed Morris. "There is so much of it here."

"Bay City used to be the center of the world for boatbuilding," says Don Comtois.

Morris and Comtois are friends, and both are members of the Bay City Historical Society. Fascinated by the maritime heritage of their community, they worked together to restore a one-of-a-kind walking-beam steamboat. "The first steel-hulled boat built on the Saginaw River [in Bay City] was a side-wheel, walking-beam steamer just like this one," Comtois says.

Their latest restoration project is not a boat, however. It's a neglected lighthouse—the 1876 Saginaw River Rear Range Light. Built during our nation's centennial year, the 68-foot brick tower is of particular historical interest. It was part of a new array of range lights—a pair of lights located some

Ed Morris and Don Comtois on board the steamboat

Saginaw River Range Light

The **Saginaw River Range Light** has an interesting history. Its beacon was among the first to be displayed in tandem with a second light to guide vessels through a narrow channel. Fifteen-year-old Dewitt Brawn, the son of a local keeper, created the range light system.

distance apart and displayed one atop the other in order to help mariners keep within a narrow channel.

The range light system now used throughout the world was the brainchild of fifteen-year-old Dewitt C. Brawn, the son of a local lighthouse keeper. Brawn had noticed how the perspective of two objects changes as the viewer moves in front of them. The Saginaw River Range Lights took advantage of this insight by displaying two lights.

"Most lighthouses warn ships away from a reef, an island, or the shoreline," says Comtois. "But a range light helps keep ships on course. You had a front range light and a rear range light. When a ship captain saw them lined up vertically one above the other, he knew his ship was safely on course—in this case toward the Saginaw River."

At Saginaw the front range light has now vanished. Only the rear range light is still standing, and it, too, is in trouble. Rendered obsolete by shifting channels and improvements in onboard navigational equipment, this light station was abandoned by the Coast Guard decades ago. It has suffered from the Great Lakes harsh winter weather and from time.

Don Comtois inside the Saginaw River Range Lighthouse

"The plaster is off the walls, and the windows are broken," Comtois says. "People look at this place and they say, 'Oh, my God!' But we don't see it that way. We see it as a labor of love, an opportunity to restore a part of our history."

In addition to Comtois and Morris, the lighthouse found a friend in Dow Chemical Company, owner of the lighthouse property. "Dow Chemical realizes this is a priceless artifact," says Morris. "Dow has taken an interest in the restoration."

Comtois and Morris hope to make the Saginaw Rear Range Light a historical rallying point for the entire Bay City community. "When it's done, it will be a place where people can come and learn about the maritime history of the Saginaw River," says Comtois. "There are people in Bay City who never knew this lighthouse existed. Now they will know how this area helped build up the country."

The Ghost Light of Presque Isle

The tallest light tower on Lake Huron stands on a pine-covered peninsula in eastern Michigan. The Presque Isle tower is 113-feet tall, and like the Presque Isle Lighthouse in Ohio, it takes its name from a strip of land that is very nearly cut off from the mainland—almost an island.

"Presque Isle is virtually an island," says Les Nichols, the manager of Presque Isle Township. "It's connected to the mainland by a small isthmus with a road. It's a great location for a lighthouse because it marks a key turning point for boats on the lake."

Built in 1870, the tall tower still has its original third-order Fresnel lens, and its beacon still guides ships on the lake. Despite its considerable age, this station is sometimes called the "New" Presque Isle Lighthouse. That is because there is an even older lighthouse about a mile away.

First lit in 1840, the "Old" Presque Isle Light once guided vessels into a small nearby harbor. But its light was extinguished long ago. Today the old lighthouse serves as a museum. Some even say the place is haunted.

Lorraine Parris has lived and worked here for almost three decades. Before she worked in the gift shop, she and her husband lived at the lighthouse as caretakers. "One night I was driving past the harbor, and I noticed a light out there in the Old Presque Isle tower," she says. "It was just as if it reached out and

New Presque Isle Lighthouse

Old Presque Isle Lighthouse

Although it is known as the **"New" Presque Isle Light,** the soaring 113-foot brick tower is more than 130 years old. The station's original third-order Fresnel lens remains in place and its beacon still guides shipping on Lake Huron.

grabbed me. I thought I must be crazy. I knew there was no light in the tower. I didn't know if it was just my imagination or what it was. But the light was there."

"I personally have seen the light," says Nichols. "I know it's there, even though the old lighthouse has not been illuminated since the new one was lit in 1870."

Nichols and Parris have not been the only ones to see the phantom light. A fogbound boater claims to have followed the light into the harbor. "He said he would never have made it in here if it hadn't been for my light," says Parris.

Perhaps Parris's most ghostly story concerns a little girl who visited Old Presque Isle with her mother during the late 1990s. The girl told Parris she had climbed the tower and met a strange man at the top.

Lorraine Parris

"What man?" asked Parris. "There's no man up there."

"Yes, there was," said the girl. "He was up there. He had a beard and I was talking to him. He told me to come back and see him again."

Then the girl pointed to a photograph over the fireplace and said, "That's the man right there." The portrait was that of Parris's husband George. Several years earlier George Parris had been struck by a major heart attack and died.

Old Presque Isle Lighthouse at night

The Old Presque Isle Lighthouse has been the setting for any number of similarly spooky stories, but most concern the tower's phantom light. More than a few locals and visitors have seen it.

"I'm not a believer in ghosts, but by golly, there is something there that makes a light," says Nichols.

"We've had the glass covered inside and the lens covered, but the light was still there," Parris says. "It seems to shine right through. There's just no way to stop it."

Well protected from waves and ice by its massive platform, the concrete-and-steel **De Tour Reef Lighthouse** was nearly impervious to the elements, but it almost succumbed to progress. Nearby channel lights made its beacon redundant, and except for the intervention of a local preservation society, the tower might have been demolished.

A Light on the Rocks

At its far northwestern end, Lake Huron narrows dramatically. As its waters become more confined, the lake confronts mariners with increased dangers. Vessels moving through this part of the lake have far less maneuvering room and far less chance of outrunning a storm. What is worse, this section of Lake Huron is chockablock with rocky islands and lurking shoals.

Several of the more threatening obstacles, such as Spectacle Reef, Poe Reef, Martin Reef, and Fourteen Foot Shoal, are marked by offshore lights. Perhaps the best known of these open water lights is the one at De Tour Reef. Ships headed for the locks at Sault Sainte

Marie are required to report their positions when they pass De Tour Reef. As a result this light has been entered in the logs of passing vessels many thousands of times.

Like its sister reef lights, the De Tour Reef beacon serves a dual purpose: It both warns mariners away from danger and guides them through the safe channel. The light station here has performed these services for the better part of a century and no doubt saved countless lives. Not many years ago, however, the lighthouse itself was in danger and needed to be saved. It has been, thanks to Bob Jones, Jeri and Chuck Feltner, and over 500 members of the De Tour Reef Light Preservation Society.

Built in 1931, the squared off concrete and steel tower stands on a massive concrete platform rising about 20 feet above the lake's surface. For many years the light was focused by a handsome Fresnel lens, but the lovely glass lens was removed after the beacon was automated in 1974. The old Fresnel is now displayed at the De Tour Village Museum on the nearby mainland.

Jeri and Chuck Feltner

Eventually the Coast Guard decided the beacon was no longer needed and announced plans to close the lighthouse. "The Coast Guard would have demolished the building if the preservation society hadn't stepped in," says Jeri Feltner.

As has been done with many other lighthouses elsewhere, the Coast Guard agreed to lease the De Tour Reef Light Station to the society. The nonprofit organization is now responsible for restoration and maintenance of the historic building.

"It's a tremendous responsibility," says Feltner. "We've signed up to preserve a really beautiful structure. De Tour Reef is an art-deco style lighthouse built in the 1930s, and just the sight of it gives you goose bumps."

As the restoration project goes forward, the lighthouse is coming back together—literally piece by piece. Some key artifacts have been located in the waters around the lighthouse. Broken or outmoded parts and machinery were sometimes dumped into the lake by construction workers or station crewmen.

Jeri Feltner talks with Alfred Lemieux.

Divers are now recovering some of these discarded items. The recovered artifacts are not just museum pieces, however. Some may be cleaned up and reused in the restored lighthouse.

Recently divers scouring the lake bottom near the light brought up a set of odd, wheel-shaped objects. At first these mysterious items could not be identified, so Feltner took them to an expert—Alfred Lemieux, age ninety-two. Lemieux was one of the workers who built the De Tour Reef Lighthouse.

"I was about twenty when I started there," says Lemieux, who is happy to pick himself out of a group photograph of lighthouse workers. "That's me right there. I'm standing on a 4-inch angle iron."

Lemieux and his fellow workers used a wide variety of tools and heavy equipment at the offshore work site, and he had little trouble identifying the wheels Feltner showed him. "They're shivs," he said. "We called them shivs, and I think they were probably from the deck crane."

Feltner enjoys meeting people like Lemieux whose personal histories are linked to the lighthouse. "Establishing relationships with people is the most rewarding thing about this effort to restore the lighthouse," says Feltner. " I am very grateful for them, and they make all the hard work very worthwhile. I'm having a great time."

Jeri Feltner's husband Chuck agrees and believes that preserving culture is an important part of the society's work. "We've developed a deeper interest in our culture," he says. "Lighthouses are a significant piece of that culture. They remind us of how we came here and what we're doing here."

Crossroads of the Lakes

A large number of the settlers who peopled the American Midwest got there by way of the Straits of Mackinac, the narrows where Lakes Huron and Michigan come together. The passage linking these two enormous lakes and separating the Upper and Lower Michigan Peninsulas is only a few miles wide. Like most constricted waterways, this one is quite dangerous. Many vessels, both large and small, have been lost here.

For sixty-five years mariners depended on the Old Mackinac Point Light to guide them safely through the straits. Established in 1892, the light shined until 1957, when the Coast Guard deactivated the lighthouse. It had been rendered obsolete by the opening of the Mackinac Bridge, which had its own navigational lights.

For Dick Campbell, the grand old stone building is more than just a decommissioned lighthouse. It was once his home. The son of a keeper, Campbell lived in lighthouses all over the Great Lakes, among them the one at Mackinac Point.

Shown here on its rear, landward side, the **Old Mackinac Point Light** once guided freighters through the key straits linking Lake Huron to Lake Michigan. Established in 1892, the station was taken out of service in 1957 after the lights on the recently completed Mackinac Bridge made its beacon unnecessary.

The lantern room at the **Old Mackinac Point Lighthouse** provides a fine view of the 3½-mile-long suspension bridge carrying motorists between the Upper and Lower Michigan Peninsulas. Considerable freighter traffic passes under the bridge's long spans.

"Old Mackinac Point Lighthouse was the cream of the crop because our family could live together twelve months a year in a village," says Campbell. "It was great. But most people probably wouldn't tolerate this sort of life today. It was too much like the military. Everything had to be in its place, and everything had to be clean. You never knew when the inspectors were coming, so you were on your toes constantly."

Campbell's family also had to put up with an inconvenience common to many light stations—the frequent droning of a powerful foghorn. "It was very loud," he says. "When we were carrying on a conversation and we would get a blast from the foghorn, we'd naturally stop. When it was over we'd continue with our conversation, but sometimes you'd lose your train of thought."

Old Mackinac Point Lighthouse

Campbell's father, a Native American, was the last keeper of the Old Mackinac Point Lighthouse. He was on hand for the November 1, 1957, opening of the Mackinac Bridge, the longest suspension bridge ever built, and afterwards began the process of closing down the light station.

"My dad had to stay here, board up the windows, and be the last one out," says Campbell. "It was a bad feeling to stand outside and watch."

Campbell also watched as Coast Guard workers dismantled the station's

Dick Campbell

fine old Fresnel lens. "As they took it apart, a lot of the pieces were thrown overboard," he says. "And others were shipped off to some unknown depot. Let's hope that someday they can find those pieces and resurrect the lighthouse."

Even without its keepers, its lens, or a light in its tower, the Old Mackinac Point Lighthouse still stands its vigil. Although it no longer guides ships, it still informs our appreciation of the past and of lighthouse keepers, both men and women, who helped open America's heartland to the world.

GULF OF MEXICO

Beacons of America's Southern Coast

The Gulf of Mexico is enormous. More than twice the size of the state of Texas, it covers some 580,000 square miles in a tossing blanket of blue-green water. And yet the Gulf is enclosed on three sides by land. This makes it more like a giant lake than an arm of the ocean and much more dangerous for mariners.

Ships are built for the open sea; they are out of their element and at great risk whenever they approach the shore. The shallows along the coasts of Florida, Alabama, Mississippi, Louisiana, and Texas are strewn with the hulks of thousands of hapless vessels that have strayed too close to land over the last 500 years. Adding to the perils of the Gulf are the vicious gales and hurricanes that swirl in from the south and east turning it into a deadly shooting gallery. It should come as no surprise then that, in a place of such troubled shores and troubled waters, lighthouses are accorded a special reverence. Here they are truly the stuff of legend.

Mae England

"Lighthouses have the appeal of structures known for saving lives," says Texas author and museum director T. Lindsay Baker.

"People are interested in tales of adventure and rescue," says Mae England, who once lived in a Florida lighthouse. "They think about the storms and how the lighthouse is there as a beacon, even during the storm."

"Lighthouses provide that ray of hope that lets you know something else is out there, and you are not the only one at sea," says Neil Hurley, a Coast Guard Reserve commander and an expert on the lighthouses of the Florida Keys.

The Dry Tortugas

The U.S. Gulf Coast stretches for 1,000 miles along the shores of five states. It is a region of deep-water ports, small fishing harbors, and inland passages, of broad estuaries and low, sandy islands. It is our "third coast," our southern coast. The Gulf coastline is anchored by a long chain of coral, sand, and limestone islands trailing southwestward from the toe of Florida. Many believe that Key West lies at the end of the chain, but it doesn't. Some 60 miles farther out into the open Gulf are the Dry Tortugas. The Dry Tortugas consist of seven tiny islands, which taken together amount to only about forty acres of land. Despite their modest size, however, the islands are a formidable threat to shipping, for they are ringed with killer reefs and sandbars.

The Gulf of Mexico is comprised of hundreds of thousands of square miles and is enclosed by land on three sides. Mariners who stray too close to the Gulf's shallow shores, are usually at great risk for harm. Gulf Coast lighthouses are especially revered for alerting sailors about the perils of the water along the coast.

"This is the last part of the chain of islands that includes the Florida Keys," says Neil Hurley, who has written a book about the Dry Tortugas and their lighthouses. "So it's an important turning point for ships crossing from the Atlantic Ocean into the Gulf of Mexico. It's also the last point of land that ships have to avoid, and it has been the site of shipwrecks reaching back to Spanish times."

Since 1826 a lighthouse has warned mariners against the dangers lurking just beneath the azure waters surrounding the islands. It was one of several built along the Gulf Coast during the 1820s.

Having acquired Florida from the Spanish in 1821, the U.S. government sought to secure the trade routes linking New Orleans and Mobile with ports on the East Coast. As a first step the navy was dispatched to the Florida Keys to flush out marauding pirates. Then

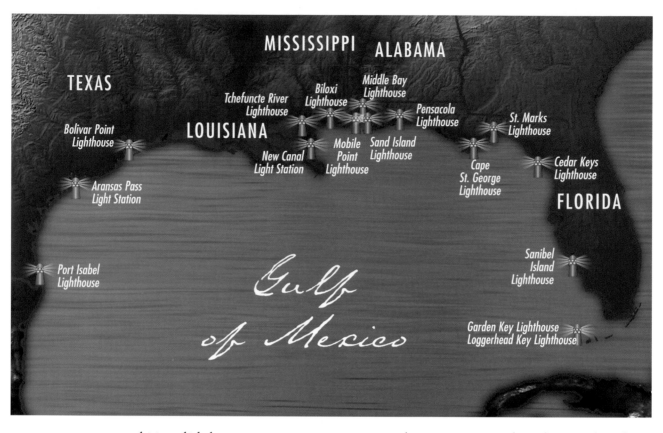

an ambitious lighthouse construction program was begun to protect ships from reefs and other natural obstacles. Eventually a nearly continuous chain of navigational lights would stretch from the Keys all the way to Texas, but it would take many decades to complete.

"The first lighthouse in the Dry Tortugas was built on Garden Key," says Hurley.

The project got under way early in 1824, but the lighthouse was not ready for service until the summer of 1826, more than a year behind schedule. Construction crews were hampered by storms, and the work suffered a severe setback when a supply ship was lost at sea. Despite the problems, however, the 70-foot conical brick tower was finally ready for service. On July 4, 1826, keeper John Flaherty lit the Garden Key lamps for the very first time. The light must have been a comforting sight for mariners.

"You're a long way from land out here," says Hurley. "Perhaps you're coming down from New Orleans and headed for an East Coast port. You've been out at sea for several days, and maybe you're

Neil Hurley

The cast-iron tower of the retired **Garden Key Lighthouse** stands atop the walls of Fort Jefferson in Florida's remote Dry Tortugas. Built in 1876, it took the place of an earlier brick tower damaged by hurricanes. The fort, lighthouse, and surrounding islands are part of the Dry Tortugas National Park.

physically tired and seasick after the battering you've taken from the waves and storms. It would have been very reassuring to see the lighthouse."

Since the islands were flat and nearly featureless, mariners approaching the Dry Tortugas during the late 1820s would have seen the tower rising out of what appeared to be open water. "It was a brick structure, and at that time there were no other buildings or houses on the island," Hurley says.

Eventually the lighthouse and its keepers would have company. To guard the strategic and the economically vital shipping channels through the Florida Straits, the U.S. Army began construction of a huge fort on Garden Key. With walls 50 feet high, 8 feet thick, and containing over forty million bricks, the enormous masonry structure eventually circled a half mile around the island. Designed for a garrison of up to 1,500 troops armed with 450 extraordinarily powerful canon, Fort Jefferson was intended to be the "Gibraltar of the Gulf." But construction of the fort, which began in 1846 and continued on and off for more than thirty years, was never completed, and none of its big canon were ever fired in defense. Before the last bricks could be laid, improvements in artillery rendered the fort's massive walls obsolete.

This view across the Fort Jefferson parade ground and walls looks west toward Loggerhead Key and its 157-foot light tower. The much taller **Loggerhead Key Lighthouse** provided a better warning for ships, particularly on the western side of the Dry Tortugas—near the most dangerous part of the turn going from the Atlantic Ocean into the Gulf of Mexico.

Outmoded by improvements in naval artillery, the 50-foot-high walls of Fort Jefferson were never completed. The arched galleries were designed for hefty smoothbore cannon, which were never fired in defense of the fort. The fort and the lighthouse on Garden Key are open to visitors who make the trek to the national park by boat or seaplane.

Today Fort Jefferson is part of the Dry Tortugas National Park. Accessible only by boat or seaplane, the park includes a pristine coral reef habitat as well as historic lighthouses and other important maritime relics. Visitors who make the trek are rewarded with one of the most isolated and pristine environments found along the U.S. coastline.

"I think the thing that is really lost today is the fact that the lighthouses were here before the fort," says Hurley. "People talk about the Dry Tortugas and they think about Fort Jefferson, but the lighthouse was here first."

Actually there have been at least three lighthouses in the Dry Tortugas, two on Garden Key and one on Loggerhead Key, about 2½ miles to the west. Only the first of these predates the fort. Its foundations can still be seen on the Fort Jefferson parade ground.

"You can see the circle of bricks, the center post, and the doorway," Hurley says. "These are the same bricks they laid during the 1820s when they built the original Dry Tortugas Lighthouse."

The lighthouse was never as effective as its designers had hoped. Its beacon was not powerful enough to cover the reefs that spread out from the islands in all directions. As a result ships and lives continued to be lost. Eventually construction of the fort would make the lighthouse all but useless. By the time the fort's walls had reached their full height, only the lantern room at the very top of the tower could be seen peeking above them. In 1873 a hurricane severely damaged the old tower, and a few years later, it was replaced by a 37-foot structure made of cast iron and boilerplate. Bolted to a granite foundation on top of the walls, this tower was active for nearly forty years. Although its light was snuffed in 1912, it still stands.

Even before the second lighthouse was built on Garden Key, mariners were demanding a better beacon for the Dry Tortugas. In 1858 the government responded by building a 157-foot brick tower on Loggerhead Key to the west of Fort Jefferson. Fitted with the most modern and powerful optic available, a first-order Fresnel lens, the new light station became a key link in the 1,000-mile-long chain of lights that were making navigation in the Gulf much easier and safer.

Loggerhead Key Lighthouse

"It was a much taller lighthouse with a much brighter light," says Hurley. "It provided a better warning for ships, particularly on the western side of the Dry Tortugas near where ships made the dangerous turn from the Atlantic into the Gulf of Mexico."

Having withstood several major hurricanes and countless squalls, the lighthouse on Loggerhead Key still stands. Its bright light remains in operation, although it is no longer as vital to shipping as was once the case. Shipboard electronics now make it possible to determine a vessel's exact position without the help of lights and channel mark-

Sunken ship near Dry Tortugas

ers. During the nineteenth century, however, seeing the Dry Tortugas Light could spell the difference between life and death for mariners.

"There were hundreds of wrecks in the Dry Tortugas area, some after the lighthouses were built," says Hurley. "But the lighthouses here certainly increased the safety of the mariner. Even today lighthouses offer important reassurance. If you're at sea, you can look out to the horizon at night and know where you are without the help of some electronic gadget."

Fish Fry at the Lighthouse

Located 120 miles north of the Dry Tortugas, the Sanibel Island Lighthouse was an important marker for ships heading for Florida's Gulf Coast. Not nearly as old as many other Florida lighthouses, it was completed in 1884. Its simple iron-skeleton design, a common one for Gulf lighthouses, was intended to allow storm winds to pass harmlessly through the tower. Nonetheless, the lighthouse suffered severe damage in a 1948 hurricane. When repairs were completed the following year, the light was automated and the last Coast Guard keeper departed for the mainland. About ten years later Charles LeBuff came to Sanibel Island and began a relationship with Sanibel Lighthouse that would last a lifetime.

"I first saw the Sanibel Light at night from 24 miles down the coast," says LeBuff. "I was out on the beach in Bonita Springs and saw this strange light on the horizon. I asked a friend what it was, and he told me it was the Sanibel Light."

A few years later LeBuff was assigned to Sanibel Island by his employers, the U.S. Fish and Wildlife Service. Along with the job went a house—one of the keeper's cottages of the Sanibel Island Lighthouse. As it turned out, LeBuff and his wife would live there for almost twenty-two years.

"I didn't look at it as anything special," says LeBuff. "It was just a place to live, and we had to pay rent. I think my rent was $9.00 a month to live in that house. Can you imagine that?"

As LeBuff can testify, however, it was not exactly like living at one of the resorts that have sprouted up on Sanibel Island in recent decades. "We had no electricity," he says. "And all we had to drink was cistern water. There was no real social life, no television, and no air-conditioning. But the worst problem in the early years were the mosquitoes. At the time Sanibel was the mosquito capital of the world."

A steel-skeleton tower with a central access cylinder, the **Sanibel Island Lighthouse** dates to 1884. This lighthouse design was popular throughout the Gulf of Mexico.

Despite the rustic living, however, LeBuff relished his life at Sanibel. "In the summertime, I chased sea turtles on the beach. In fact I started a sea turtle conservation program. I played a lot of cards and did a lot of writing. It was a much different lifestyle."

In the early 1960s the outside world dramatically intruded on the peaceful isolation of Sanibel Island. A causeway was built, linking the island to the mainland. "The causeway came in May of 1963, and it changed this place forever. It's still a wonderful place, but it'll never be the same. Fifty years ago people came here to shell, to bird-watch, to write books, to retreat. Today, for many people, Sanibel is just another Florida resort destination. People come here to play tennis, play golf, and maybe go sight-seeing. But they still get turned on by the seashells on the beaches—still get that Sanibel stoop."

Charles LeBuff

When Charles LeBuff retired after thirty-two years with the U.S. Fish and Wildlife Service, he wrote a book about his life on the island and his time at the lighthouse. As part of the project, LeBuff sought assistance from people who knew even more than he did about the Sanibel Lighthouse—former keepers and their families.

Sanibel Island Lighthouse

Among those LeBuff contacted were Bob and Mae England, who had lived at the lighthouse for a few years. Bob was the station's last official Coast Guard keeper.

"It was just another island," Mae recalls. "And I was just living in this big old white house by the beach. The only thing special about it was the fact that you had to stay there. It was a nice house, of course, and I liked the water, the beach, and the shells. I also like to fish.

"One time I saw the fish working out there and I took my casting net and ran down and threw it out over a bunch and got thirty-two fish," she recalls. "Bob would go up the island and say, 'Fish fry at the lighthouse, fish fry at the lighthouse.' And we had a big fish fry and invited everybody on the island," she chuckles. "That was a good time."

Mae and Margaret England, looking at photos of their days at the lighthouse.

Not all occasions on Sanibel were so lighthearted. The England family weathered any number of damaging squalls. England's daughter, Margaret, recalls a hurricane. "I can remember the high water and things hitting the bottom of the house. I guess that would be something for a little girl to remember."

Margaret helps her mother preserve the family history from their brief time living at the Sanibel Lighthouse. They have a rich collection of photos—and memories.

While she takes a very personal view of the lighthouse, Mae England recognizes its importance to the safety of mariners. "The lighthouse is there as a beacon. Have you ever been out there in the Gulf in the dark? It's real nice to know where you're going. That light goes 30 miles out there, and that's a good thing."

LeBuff agrees. He also thinks the beacon has much to offer the local landlubbers. "I think everyone who comes home across that bridge to Sanibel at night is attracted to the lighthouse. You see the light and get that special feeling of home calling to you. I think as long as we can insist and the Coast Guard agrees, we should keep that light burning."

Laboratory at a Lighthouse

University of Florida Professor Jon Fajans often brings students to explore the waters around the Cedar Keys National Wildlife Refuge. Their hands-on research experience is part of a study program offered by the Seahorse Key Marine Laboratory.

"The laboratory was established here in the mid-1950s," says Fajans. "It provides an excellent opportunity for University of Florida faculty and students to study the marine environment. There's a lot of diversity out here, things that aren't found onshore."

The students eat, sleep, and work in one of the most unique labs and dormitories found on any college campus—the Cedar Keys Lighthouse. Since 1953 the lighthouse has played its current role as an offshore educational center, but it was once an

Jon Fajans

important navigational station. Its beacon guided countless lumber freighters that came here to take on loads of hardwood, much of it for use in the manufacture of pencils.

A modest, one-story brick dwelling with a small tower on its roof, the Cedar Keys Lighthouse was built on Seahorse Key in 1854. Its designer was army engineer George

Modest by comparison to other Gulf lighthouses built by U.S. Army Lieutenant of Engineers George G. Meade, the **Cedar Keys Lighthouse** has a tower only 28-feet high. It was built in 1854 to foster the local timber industry—lumber freighters came here to collect cedar hardwood that was used in the manufacture of pencils. Located in the Cedar Keys National Wildlife Refuge, it now serves as an educational center and marine laboratory for the University of Florida.

Meade, who would later win fame during the Civil War as a Union general. Although the lighthouse was only 28-feet tall, it stood on a sandy hillock. This raised the focal plane of its fourth-order beacon to 75 feet above sea level and gave it a range of approximately 15 miles. Completed for a bargain price of only $12,000, the little lighthouse served mariners for more than sixty years. With lumbering and other local commerce on the decline, the light station was permanently closed in 1915.

Although it stood empty for many years, the station is once again a lively place. "The students really enjoy it here," says Fajans. "It's certainly different from any kind of dorm room they've experienced before."

The young visitors learn much about the ocean and the myriad creatures inhabiting the refuge. The island is home to as many as ten different species of ibis and up to 10,000 breeding pairs of egret. But the students also learn about the history of the lighthouse.

"We make a point of impressing the history on our students," Fajans says. "They like to hear stories about the lighthouse, and they certainly like to make up a few stories of their own."

Because of the university presence on Seahorse Key, the lighthouse and the history it represents are being preserved. As part of its lease agreement with the U.S. Fish and Wildlife Service, the university takes care of routine maintenance on the building.

"The easiest way to maintain the building is through our partnership

Students enjoying the view from the Cedar Keys gallery.

with the University of Florida," says Cedar Keys refuge manager Ken Litzenberger. "Without them, it would be difficult."

The arrangement frees up refuge funds for use in wildlife conservation. "That's the main purpose of the refuge," says Litzenberger. "Barrier islands like this are especially important for tropical songbirds that fly from South America to nest."

But Litzenberger also sees the lighthouse as an important resource— a cultural resource. The university and its students are helping him protect it. "It's a good marriage, a win-win situation," he says. "The University of Florida uses the lighthouse for environmental education, marine science, and research. So they have bodies out here to help protect and maintain the historic resources."

The professors and their students believe they are the primary beneficiaries. "This experience allows us to immerse the students in the environment," says

Ken Litzenberger

Fajans. "It allows them to completely focus on what we are teaching in class—to wake up, take a look around, and see what's really there."

Its keeper's residence nearly hidden by the lush coastal growth, the stark white tower of the **St. Marks Lighthouse** rises above marshy ground near the mouth of a Florida river. Earlier lighthouses here fell victim to war and erosion, but this one has survived since 1867. The station still guides local fishermen and also helps attract visitors to a national wildlife refuge.

Lighthouse Refuge

To the north of Cedars Keys, the coastline bends toward the west and the Florida panhandle region. Near the sharpest point in the bend is another pristine natural area, the St. Marks National Wildlife Refuge. Like the Cedar Keys Refuge, this one is also home to a historic lighthouse.

"Lighthouse Road is the main road through the refuge," says ranger Robin Will, who has worked here for over twenty years. "It's a 7-mile wildlife drive that starts at the visitor center and goes all the way down to the end of the road at the old St. Marks Lighthouse. Along the way people get to see a variety of habitats, including pine forests, open salt marshes, and vast fresh water marshes full of alligators, ducks, birds, and other wildlife. So this drive is a great way to introduce people to the refuge."

But people don't just come here to see the animals. "The big attraction for everyone at the end of the road is the St. Marks Lighthouse," Will says. "It's a national historic site and a well-loved landmark. People come from all over the world to see it. It's still a working rear range light and you can park right in front of it."

The St. Marks Light still guides mariners just as it has for more than 170 years, but the tower seen today is not quite that old. The first lighthouse was built in 1831, but its workmanship was so poor that government inspectors had it torn down. A second tower lasted only until 1840, when it was undercut by erosion. A third St. Marks tower was blown up by Confederate raiders during the Civil War. The existing structure, completed in 1867, is actually the station's fourth lighthouse. Erected on a deep limestone foundation, its 4-foot-thick walls are 82 feet tall.

"The lighthouse was put here to guide ships into the mouth of the St. Marks River," Will says. "Back during the early 1800s, St. Marks was a booming shipping port. At that time, Florida's only railroad came right through Tallahassee and down into St. Marks. It brought all kinds of stores and supplies that went out on the big boats."

Ranger Robin Will at St. Marks National Wildlife Refuge

A bobcat on the prowl

The constantly shifting shoals and sandbars near the mouth of the river caused many wrecks, but the St. Marks beacon made navigating the river entrance easier and safer. No doubt its guiding light prevented the loss of many vessels and lives.

"The lighthouse is a part of our history that fascinates people," says Will, but she is quick to point out that the St. Marks refuge itself is also historic. "Established in 1931 primarily for migratory birds, it is one of the oldest preserves in our national system."

Located about 25 miles south of the state capital of Tallahassee, in an area known as the "Big Bend" region of Florida, the refuge has much to offer visitors. "This is a really nice undeveloped, pristine, natural part of the state," says Will. "The refuge wraps around Apalachee Bay, a very shallow estuary. The bay has 41 miles of coastline and lots of fish, so it's a great place to come fishing."

The wildlife on land is also abundant. "We have over 6,000 alligators, and lots of birds," Will says. "You might see wading birds, great egrets, great blue herons, or little green herons. You might see coots

Established in 1931, the St. Marks National Wildlife Refuge is one of the oldest federal preserves. It consists largely of coastal marshlands and forest. Alligators are easily spotted on a 7-mile wildlife drive along Lighthouse Road, which terminates at the St. Marks Lighthouse.

and ducks if you come during the fall and winter months. You might see white-tail deer feeding, bobcats crossing the road, or maybe a Florida black bear sneaking through the palm meadows."

Will encourages park visitors to slow down so they can appreciate all this natural wealth. "I definitely hope that those lighthouse fans who drive all the way into the refuge will leave thinking what a special place this is and that it isn't just the lighthouse that makes it special. I hope they take with them a "wildlife moment"—a bald eagle feeding its young, an alligator sliding into the marsh, or a dolphin leaping in the bay."

For Will there have been countless moments of this sort. "This has always been a special place for me. I enjoy just listening to the marsh sounds and being next to the lighthouse and feeling part of all the years that have gone by."

Leaning Tower of the Gulf

Roughly half way along its 200-mile length, the Florida panhandle pushes southward into the Gulf forming a bump of land large enough to be noticed on any map. This is an area known as the "forgotten coast." Its hub is Apalachicola, one of Florida's oldest towns.

"This is just a phenomenal place to live," says John Lee, general manager of the *Apalachicola Times*. Lee has been with the newspaper for more than twenty years. "This is the oyster capital of the world, and the shrimp, crab, clams that come out of this area are wonderful. The Apalachicola Bay oyster is the best in the world. Period."

As Lee is quick to point out, the region's charm is not limited to its world-class seafood. It has other wonders as well, and one of these is a lighthouse.

Lee first encountered the Cape St. George

John Lee

Lighthouse during the early 1960s when he was stationed at Apalachicola with the air force. "We used to fish off the outside of the island, and I'd come in from a late day of fishing and see the tower with its blinking light."

At the time he never dreamed that he was to play an important role in the survival of this historic landmark. In fact, decades would pass before he realized the old lighthouse was in serious trouble. In 1995, after Hurricane Opal, Lee and a *Times* photographer were exam-

ining storm damage on the barrier islands off Apalachicola. At Cape St. George they were confronted with an astonishing sight.

"The lighthouse was leaning out over the water at an angle of maybe seven degrees," says Lee. "We did a joke photograph that showed me pretending to push up the lighthouse."

Later this photograph would become part of a promotion aimed at rescuing the leaning lighthouse. An advertisement in the *Times* put questions to the public. Could the tower be saved? How? And how much would it cost?

"We ran the advertisement a couple of times and got responses from all over the United States," Lee says.

Encouraged by the groundswell of interest, Lee formed a nonprofit organization called the Cape St. George Lighthouse Society. Under its slogan "Save the Light," the society started collecting donations, some as large as $10,000. The restoration effort was expected to cost millions, however, and the society had little hope of being able to raise such large sums. Clearly an innovative approach would be required.

Bill Grimes and John Lee

"The pundits said it wasn't possible, that it was a multimillion-dollar deal," says Lee. "But then we talked to a gentleman named Bill Grimes."

A Tallahassee general contractor who specializes in difficult projects, Grimes thought the job could be done for far less than the original estimates, perhaps for as little as $200,000.

"John and I go back a long way," says Grimes. "And I wanted to do this badly enough that I was willing to take it on a shoestring."

After a survey of the work site, Grimes realized he had taken on a big job. "The first time I saw the lighthouse," he says, " it was sitting on four massive brick piers and leaning to the south and west at seven or eight degrees."

What was worse, the condition of the building was rapidly deteriorating. When Grimes made his next visit, he found that the brick piers had washed away, leaving the tower teetering precariously on the sand.

"I never doubted that we could save the lighthouse," Grimes says. "The question was could we get it done before the storms came."

In a race against time, Grimes and his crew set to work. They had difficulty getting materials to the site, a low barrier island about 8 miles from the mainland. But they had to move quickly and get as much done as possible before the next big gale or hurricane struck the coast. A really big storm might damage the tower beyond repair.

Undercut by beach erosion, the once leaning tower of the **Cape St. George Lighthouse** was saved from collapse by a privately funded restoration effort. Local volunteers decided not to move the lighthouse from its original location at the edge of the Gulf of Mexico.

Although waves lap at the base of the structure and nearby sands continue to erode, the **Cape St. George** tower stands straight on its new pilings.

The nineteenth-century construction crews that built the light station in the first place had grappled with similar problems—a tight budget, a remote site, and unpredictable weather. The original Cape St. George Lighthouse was built in 1833 by legendary contractor Winslow Lewis, a former sea captain. For just $9,500, Lewis managed to build a 72-foot brick tower and equip it with a lamp and reflector lighting system he had designed himself.

This no-frills Lewis lighthouse proved inadequate from the start, and in 1852 it was replaced with the structure that, thanks to Grimes, Lee, and others, still stands today. The tower successfully weathered nearly 150 years of storm winds and hurricane-driven flood tides. But the sands of Gulf Coast barrier islands are constantly shifting, and by the 1990s erosion had almost become its undoing.

To stabilize the structure, Grimes and his workers drove forty new pilings, each 15 feet in length, along the base of the tower. Then some 70 cubic yards of concrete were added to provide extra weight. To fight erosion, 115 feet of vinyl sheeting was laid out around the exterior to create a buffer against wave action. These protective measures have apparently succeeded.

"I feel very confident that the lighthouse will be here for a long time" says Grimes. "It's a satisfying legacy, being the ones who were able to save it."

Lee also takes pride in this accomplishment. "If the right people hadn't been at the right place at the right time, there's no question in my mind that there would no longer be a Cape St. George Lighthouse. It's a part of Americana. It's saved lives, and I take a lot of pride in the fact that we were able to save it for future generations."

Pensacola's Navy Light

Well to the west of Apalachicola, near the border with Alabama, Florida's best preserved lighthouse continues to serve the purpose for which it was built. Located on the Pensacola Naval Air Station, the lofty tower still marks the entrance to Pensacola Bay, a body of water long frequented by U.S. fighting ships.

As early as 1820, just after the acquisition of Florida from Spain, the U.S. Navy was ordered into the Gulf to quell piracy. To keep its warships well supplied and ready for battle, the navy established a base at Pensacola, which offered a deep-water port. The first lighthouse was built in 1824 to guide the navy's battle fleet and supply ships into the bay.

Like the original tower at Cape St. George, the first Pensacola Lighthouse was the work of Winslow Lewis. For a modest price of $5,725, Lewis provided a 45-foot high tower fitted with an oil lamp and reflector system of his own design. The lighthouse turned out to be something less than a bargain, however, and was never considered adequate by the mariners forced to depend on it. By 1859 it had been replaced by a soaring, 150-foot tower equipped with the latest in optical technology at the time—a powerful first-order Fresnel lens. That second tower still stands.

The soaring 150-foot **Pensacola Lighthouse** dominates its lovely nineteenth-century keeper's residence. Located on the Pensacola Navel Air Station, this is one of Florida's best-preserved and most accessible lighthouses.

"The Pensacola Lighthouse is very well preserved," says Tom Garner, a lifelong resident of Pensacola and author of a historical book about its lighthouse. "It has many of its original outbuildings, including the keeper's quarters, the oil house, and a two-story workroom attached to the base of the tower."

Many lighthouses long ago lost their residences and other support buildings, along with the interesting historical insights these structures could offer. "We're very fortunate our lighthouse still has its outbuildings," says Garner.

The Pensacola Lighthouse offers another big plus to lighthouse lovers and history buffs. Its huge, chandelierlike Fresnel lens remains in place. "We're fortunate to have the original lens. A lot of these lenses, the first-order lenses especially, have been removed."

Garner takes a special interest in the big crystal lenses. "Fresnel lenses are fantastic," he says. "They were handpolished by the makers in France."

In Garner's eye the big Pensacola lens is a true work of art. "It's huge, something like 9-feet tall and 6 feet in diameter," he says. "I'm always impressed to see it at night. It radiates beams, like spokes on a wheel or a crown, and they shine out over the land and water. It's a magnificent sight, like the glow of a diamond."

Pensacola's impressive first-order Fresnel lens focuses the station's beacon just as efficiently today as it did when it was installed during the nineteenth century.

Mariners may take a more practical view of the lens and the bright beacon it focuses. They rely on it for guidance. The extraordinary concentrating power of the lens can make the light visible from as much as 27 miles away, and the considerable height of the tower gives the light a longer reach. Since the tower stands on a 40-foot bluff, the tower places the focal plane of its beacon 190 feet above sea level. That makes it the tallest remaining tower on the Gulf, and for anyone able or willing to climb the tower's 177 steps, it provides a tremendous view.

Tom Garner

"I think one of the things that drives people's fascination for lighthouses is the view from the top," says Garner. "I've climbed the Pensacola tower countless times over the years, and I never get tired of it—but of course I do get out of breath."

Garner knows the experience is well worth the considerable effort of the climb. "You open up that door to the outside and break out into sunlight, and it is the most awesome, breathtaking view you're ever going to see. It's the best view in Pensacola."

Lights over Mobile Bay

Of the five states washed by the waters of the Gulf, Alabama has the shortest ocean shoreline. Yet no other Gulf Coast state can claim a body of water equal to Mobile Bay. The 27-mile long bay was the first important commercial harbor on the Gulf of Mexico, and even today it remains a key destination for ships.

Historically only a few lighthouses have marked the shores of Alabama, and nearly all were built to guide shipping into or around Mobile Bay. Among these was the Mobile Point Lighthouse located on a spit of land marking the east side of the crucial entrance to the bay.

Immediately after the U.S. took possession of Alabama from the Spanish in 1821, a fort was built here to establish control over the region. The following year a small brick light tower was erected on the parade ground of the new fort. It was manned by a soldier paid a few extra dollars each month to keep the light burning. This early beacon was never very effective, and the light could rarely be seen from more than 10 miles away. When Union Admiral David Farragut forced his way into Mobile during the Civil War, his gunboats blasted the fort and, along with it, the lighthouse.

A simple iron tower replaced the original brick **Mobile Point Lighthouse** blasted to rubble by the guns of Admiral Farragut's fleet during the battle of Mobile Bay. Returned to service in 1873, the light guided mariners until it was deactivated almost a century later. It is Alabama's only accessible lighthouse structure.

In 1873 the shattered Mobile Point Lighthouse was replaced by a stark, black, steel tower erected on the broken and battered walls of the fort. The 35-foot metal building held a fourth-order Fresnel lens and displayed a red light.

Having served faithfully for almost a century, the little lighthouse was finally shut down in 1966. Today the important job of marking the bay entrance is handled by a rotating aeronautical beacon atop a slender 125-foot tower. Located just outside the walls of the fort, this modern structure is more suggestive of a radio broadcast tower than a lighthouse. Although no longer in operation, the old 1873 tower remains on display at the Fort Morgan State Historic Site. It is Alabama's only accessible lighthouse.

Fort Morgan visitors who look southeast toward the open waters of the Gulf will be treated to a view of another historic structure, the Sand Island Lighthouse. Its giant 132-foot brick tower was built in 1871 on a small, wave-swept island about 4 miles offshore. It was Alabama's only coastal light, and mariners headed for Mobile Bay were guided by its powerful first-order beacon.

Warren Lee

Today it is a lighthouse under siege. The huge tower no longer stands on dry land, and its walls and foundation are constantly exposed to the Gulf. In 1906 a hurricane carried away much of the tiny island and, along with it, the station's keeper and his wife. Their bodies were never found. Later storms swallowed up the keeper's residence and what remained of the island. For many years now, the Gulf has threatened to claim the tower itself.

"The tower now sits amid a man-made island of rocks," says Warren Lee, who has researched the lighthouse and is working along with others to save it. "If we don't do something soon, we're going to lose this great monument to our past."

Over the years loads of massive stones have been ferried out and piled around the tower to protect it from the Gulf's destructive waves. Little else has been done, however, and the tower has continued to deteriorate. Lee hopes this trend can be reversed and the historic lighthouse restored.

"For fifty years now, the tower has been more or less neglected," he says. "But it is on the National Register of Historic Places and is certainly worth saving."

Lee's personal connection to the lighthouse has deep roots, reaching back into his childhood. "When I was a kid, my family used to spend summers out there. I have a lot of warm childhood memories associated with the lighthouse."

Others are now joining his effort to preserve the tower. But saving it won't be easy. "One of the unique things about this lighthouse is also one of the things that's making it hard to save. It's located well offshore. You can't just drive your car out there and walk up in the tower."

If the lighthouse succumbs, it will become the third, and probably the last, of Sand Island's fallen towers. The first, built in 1838, was torn down and replaced by an impressive 150-foot brick structure designed by innovative army engineer Thomas Leadbetter. Completed in 1859, this second tower stood for little more than two years before being

With the surrounding land long ago swept away by hurricanes, Alabama's **Sand Island Lighthouse** is under siege by the Gulf and in danger of collapse. An artificial island of rock offers some protection, but the tower has deteriorated markedly since it was abandoned in 1971.

blown up by a Confederate raiding party to keep it out of the hands of a Union blockade fleet. Ironically the raiders reported their success to none other than Leadbetter, by then a Confederate officer and government official.

The sun sets behind the **Sand Island Lighthouse** near the entrance to Mobile Bay. The threatened tower has friends who hope to save it, but restoration efforts will be difficult and costly. "One of the things that's making it hard for us in the battle to save it is the fact that it's offshore," says Warren Lee.

Sand Island's third lighthouse has survived far longer than its predecessors, more than one and a quarter centuries, in fact, but its future is far from secure. Some consider it among our nation's most endangered lighthouses.

Well within the confined waters of Mobile Bay stands another threatened Alabama lighthouse. Its name describes its location. "The Middle Bay Lighthouse really is in the middle of Mobile Bay," says Hal Pierce. "It's way out there."

A hexagonal, Chesapeake Bay cottage-style structure, the Middle Bay Lighthouse looks quite out of place poised over the shallows near the Deep South city of Mobile. The two-story building rests on iron pilings that were screwed into the muddy bottom of the bay when this station was established in 1885. During and after construction, the screw piles sank an additional 7 feet into the soft mud, leaving the lighthouse shorter than originally planned. Even so, it served mariners efficiently for more than eighty years, marking a key turning point for ships headed toward Mobile.

Deactivated in 1967, the unusual structure might have been demolished, if not for the efforts of lighthouse friends like Pierce. A retired navy captain, Pierce serves as chairman of the Middle Bay Lighthouse Commission, which oversees the care and maintenance of the old building.

While much of the commission's funding comes from the state, the majority of work at the lighthouse is done by volunteers. "We have a very large group, and they like to come out here and work," Pierce says. "They paint and fix, and they do it all for nothing. The people that work on this lighthouse have an amazing spirit."

As a former seaman Pierce understands better than most the critical role lighthouses once played in the lives of mariners. "I spent thirty-one years in the navy," he says. "At times lighthouses were extremely important to me."

Although their importance to navigation has been diminished by advances in technology, lighthouses remain a vital link to the past. "They are a commentary on our history," Warren Lee says. "This lighthouse witnessed a time when there were no interstates. People can't even imagine it now, but back then all your goods had to come by ship. Lighthouses are a living reminder of those times."

Though few in number and jeopardized by time, neglect, and the elements, the lighthouses of Alabama remain impressive symbols of the state's maritime heritage. "We feel these lighthouses represent our history," Lee says. "That is why we must save them."

Anchored securely by screw piles, Mobile's cottage-style **Middle Bay Lighthouse** has survived storms and flooding tides for more than a century. Although no longer active, it is considered an important symbol of Alabama's maritime heritage.

Hal Pierce

Where Men Fear to Tread

Mississippi was never a major shipping destination. The state's coastal waters were too shallow and circuitous for large vessels, so most of the Gulf's commercial maritime traffic went elsewhere. Even so, ships moving eastward or westward along the dangerous Mississippi coast needed all the navigational assistance they could get, and at one time, more than a dozen lighthouses marked the chain of low, sandy barrier islands that lay just offshore. Today only one Mississippi lighthouse remains intact, and it has a most peculiar location.

"The Biloxi Lighthouse stands right in the middle of four lanes of traffic," says Lolly Barnes. "It's in the middle of Highway 90, or Beach Boulevard as it's called here in Biloxi. So if you're driving along the Mississippi Gulf coast, you're sure to see our lighthouse."

Barnes is the historical administrator for the city of Biloxi. "The lighthouse is one of our premier landmarks," she says. "Everyone here in Biloxi and along the coast is very proud of it."

Many light towers are located on remote islands or promontories where they are less likely to be noticed, but the Biloxi Lighthouse could hardly have a higher profile. "It's very visible," says Barnes. "When you think of lighthouses, you think of them out on a windswept

Active since 1847, the **Biloxi Lighthouse** today stands in a median between the east-and-westbound lanes of busy Highway 90. The tower is open daily for tours.

island. But our lighthouse is right here in the community. It's seen every day by people who live here and by visitors. So it's really at the center of things in Biloxi. It's also the historical heart of the city."

The white, 48-foot tower is a historical treasure. "In 1847 Congress allocated $12,000 to build a lighthouse here," says Barnes. "The Murray & Hazelhurst Company constructed the lighthouse in Baltimore, Maryland, and shipped it to Biloxi. It's an iron tower with a brick interior."

The history of the Biloxi Lighthouse is enriched by the fact that several of its keepers were women. "The female keepers add to the historic interest of the light," says Barnes. "The first keeper was a gentleman, but his successor was Mary Reynolds, who kept the light throughout the Civil War period."

Reynolds retired in 1866. The next keeper was a man named Perry Younguns, who died after only a year of service. Following Younguns's death, his wife Maria was appointed keeper, a post she held for more than half a century. When she retired after fifty-three years, her daughter Miranda became keeper.

"We are very proud of the history of female keepers here," Barnes says. "Mary Reynolds is a role model. There's a letter that she wrote to the governor concerning her struggles as keeper—going out in storms to keep the light burning, going out where, as she described it, 'men fear to tread.'"

The lighthouse is quite popular with

Now automated, the fifth-order **Biloxi Light** still glows brightly. This Mississippi light station is famous for its female keepers, especially the fearless Mary Reynolds.

children, especially girls. "I have a young niece who pleaded with me to get her up in the tower," says Barnes, who enhanced her status as an aunt by offering her niece a personal tour. "We were able to go to the top and enjoy the beautiful view of the islands and the city. It was really something very magical."

Lolly Barnes

Recognizing the importance of the lighthouse as a symbol for the community, Biloxi has included an image of the tower on its city logo. "We have the lighthouse and a shrimp on the Biloxi logo," says Barnes. "That says so much about our history as a maritime community. And so does the lighthouse. It's living history, really. It gives you a sense of stepping back in time and experiencing what our community was like in the 1850s."

As Barnes sees it, the lighthouse has made an indelible mark on Biloxi. It is hard for her to think of one without the other. "I grew up just a few blocks from the lighthouse," she says. "And it has always been a part of my life, a part of Biloxi."

Lights Down in the Delta

The coast of Louisiana is very much unlike that of the other states bordering the Gulf of Mexico. It consists mostly of delta country built up by silt brought from faraway plains and mountains by the Mississippi River. Here a timeless tug-of-war between land and water has produced a swampy netherworld of marshes, lakes, rivers, and bayous. Louisiana's ever-changing shoreline creates special challenges for mariners.

Few of the lighthouses here were built to mark Louisiana's outer Gulf Coast. Most were designed to help mariners navigate the state's shallow and often serpentine inland waterways.

Louisiana's only intact, operating lighthouse is located on Lake Pontchartrain near the fabled city of New Orleans. A 50-foot tall, square wooden building with a lantern and gallery rising through its roof, the New Canal Lighthouse was built more than a century ago. Its light still guides mariners, but that is no longer the primary function of this lighthouse, which now serves as home for Coast Guard Station New Orleans.

The station keeps watch over a large area. "We're responsible for approximately 7,500 square miles of the Mississippi and the bayous south of the Mississippi," says Chief Warrant Officer Frank Kratochvil, who has twenty-two years of service in the U.S. Coast Guard. "We are also responsible for Lake Pontchartrain, which is 25 miles by 48 miles and is crossed by the longest bridge in the world."

Established in 1838, the **New Canal Light** still guides vessels along the southern shore of Lake Ponchartrain. Over the years, several different light towers served here. The existing light-house is about a century old and for many years has doubled as a U.S. Coast Guard station.

RECREATING FALLEN TOWERS

As many of Louisiana's lighthouses become distant memories, the beauty of these once elegant structures is being preserved in the artistry of New Orleans painter Peter Briant. He has painted many of the lighthouses that once stood near New Orleans.

A native of New Orleans, Briant studied architecture at Tulane University and art at the University of Southern Mississippi. He started his career doing architectural renderings in Los Angeles.

"I've pretty much been painting all my life," he says. "And most of my subjects have been architectural. I love architectural details."

Nowadays Briant uses old photographs, drawings, and extensive research to meticulously recreate the state's fallen towers. "It's a shame, but there are a lot of lighthouses in this area that no longer stand," says Briant. "I'm trying to bring them back, to paint them the way they were."

Artist Peter Briant

Many other Louisiana light stations have become rundown or have changed dramatically in appearance. Briant paints them as they appeared during their glory days. He has painted the Rigolets Lighthouse, for example, as it looked during its active years, and the Tchefuncte River Lighthouse in Madisonville as it looked before the keeper's dwelling was relocated.

Briant may spend fifteen hours on a painting and even longer if he's concentrating on precision and including even the most minute details. A softer, more romantic painting including fewer details may take less time. "I'm really into the details," says Briant. "But a lot of people think of lighthouses as very romantic."

Briant is happy to share both the romance and detail of old lighthouses with the public. "When I do shows and exhibits, the lighthouse paintings get snapped up pretty fast," he says.

The **Tchefuncte River Lighthouse** as remembered in one of Peter Briant's paintings.

Those on duty here must remain constantly vigilant, for the shallow lake can be a dangerous place. "Pontchartrain is only about 15 feet deep, and when the wind kicks up it can get pretty nasty out there. We've experienced 8- to 10-foot seas out there, and that's pretty big for a lake."

Since 1838, when the station's first tower was built, mariners on the lake have looked to the New Canal Light for guidance. The lighthouse got its name from a canal that was supposed to link Pontchartrain with the bustling Mississippi River docks several miles from the lake. The canal project was never completed, but the lighthouse put here to mark the canal's Pontchartrain entrance remained. Rebuilt in 1855 and again during the 1890s, the old lakeside sentinel still stands.

It became a Coast Guard station in 1969. "There's so much history here," says Kratochvil. "Unfortunately the station is moving to a much bigger building. We do need the room, but I think everybody's going to miss this place because of its unique history." (The Coast Guard did move in June 2001, but continues to use the New Canal Station.)

The New Canal Light Station has seen many changes over the years. The lighthouse was once located well out in the lake, about a quarter of a mile from

The rooftop tower and lantern room of the New Canal Lighthouse near New Orleans

U.S. Coast Guard Chief Warrant Officer Frank Kratochvil

shore. But today, after a century of landfill projects, it's onshore. Another big change came when the station's classical fifth-order Fresnel lens was removed and exchanged for the modern optic that now provides the beacon.

"The light is still there," says Kratochvil. "But it's no longer a prominent aide to navigation. It's kind of hard to see with all the background lights."

Many of Louisiana's other lighthouses have been severely damaged or lost due to neglect and bad weather. Among the broken-down survivors is the solitary tower of the Port

The abandoned tower of the Port Ponchartrain Lighthouse

Rigolets Lighthouse

Pontchartrain Light, located on private land not far from the New Canal Lighthouse. Built in 1855, the 40-foot masonry tower once marked a busy port, but now it is an empty, abandoned shell. Like its neighbor, the Port Pontchartrain Light originally stood far offshore, but landfill projects eventually surrounded it with dry land.

Another of Louisiana's neglected lighthouses sits in the marshes of Lake Pontchartrain in an area known as the Rigolets. Built during the 1850s, the wooden structure was abandoned more than half a century ago. Remarkably, the light still stands, having survived decades of high water, hurricanes, and no regular maintenance.

The Rigolets Lighthouse is haunted by history. Keeper Tom Harrison was killed here in 1862 during a raid by Confederate militiamen. Believed to be a Union sympathizer, he was the only Lighthouse Service keeper known to have been killed in the line of duty during the Civil War.

To the northwest of the Rigolets is the bucolic town of Madisonville. Here a light station established during the 1830s remains in operation.

"Ours is a very nice little town," says Colleen Collier Fields, considered by many to be Madisonville's unofficial historian. "If it didn't exist, Norman Rockwell would have made it up. It has a justice of the peace, a barber, and a mayor who runs the local drive-in hamburger stand."

When Fields moved to Madisonville twenty-five years ago, it had about 400 residents. Now it has 8,000, but the town has never lost its quaint charm. Even so, Madisonville does have its own still active lighthouse, a distinction many larger and more active shore communities cannot claim.

In 1837 the government established a light station here at the mouth of the Tchefuncte River. The beacon was considered strategic, since it marked the river entrance and was located directly across Lake Pontchartrain from New Orleans. The station's first tower, a squat, 38-foot brick structure, was burned during the Civil War. The existing 43-foot brick-and-stone tower dates to 1867.

For a decade Fields lived in the station keeper's cottage, which no longer stands beside the old tower. Damaged by a hurricane, the bungalow-style dwelling was moved 2 miles inland and thoroughly restored. "They brought it upriver on a barge and put it where it is today," Fields says.

The tower of the Tchefuncte River Lighthouse has not been so fortunate. Weather and vandalism have taken a heavy toll on the structure. Even so, it still helps boats find the difficult river entrance, and it remains an important symbol for a town still closely linked to Louisiana's waterways.

"The town is right on the river" says Fields. "Our town hall faces the river, the best local restaurants all face the river, and all of our local events take place on the river. Ours is the only deep-water river on the lake, and historically we've been an important shipbuilding town. The shipyard right in back of us built ships that were used in World War I and World War II."

Madisonville was also the place where a small flotilla of American gunboats gathered before taking on a powerful British fleet during the Battle of New Orleans. The British used their heavy guns to smash the overmatched American vessels before landing an invasion force bent on capturing New Orleans. Later Andrew Jackson's ragtag army drove the British back in a famous victory that preserved U.S. control of Louisiana and the Mississippi.

Nowadays Madisonville is better known for fishing boats and sailing yachts than for warships. "Madisonville has become a sports paradise," says Fields. "Since the lake is shallow, boaters rely on the lighthouse to help them stay in the channel and guide them safely into the river."

Proud of their lighthouse and conscious of the role it continues to play in local commerce, the people of Madisonville are determined to preserve their historic lighthouse. "We have a really good committee right now attached to our local maritime museum," says Fields. "The committee is in the process of cleaning, painting, and restoring the lighthouse."

The tower of the **Tchefuncte River Lighthouse** near Madisonville, Louisiana, dates to 1867. The keeper's cottage was moved down river many years ago. This rear-range light continues to serve pleasure boaters and fishermen as both a day and night marker.

"Queen of the Waves"

T exas has the longest shoreline of any state on the Gulf of Mexico. Stretching more than 400 miles from Louisiana to Mexico, the Texas coast can be a dangerous place for ships. Countless vessels have fallen victim here to hidden reefs, shifting sand-bars, and treacherous shoals. To warn mariners against these perils, Texas once had as many as fifty lighthouses, but furious storms, a constantly shifting coast, and years of neglect have reduced the number to a mere handful.

T. Lindsay Baker

Bolivar Point Lighthouse

"The most striking thing about the Texas coast is its sameness—the low barrier islands and flat terrain with no obvious landmarks," says Lindsay Baker. "It's very easy to get lost along the Texas coast, and that is why we needed lighthouses. They provide a vertical element in an otherwise horizontal landscape."

T. Lindsay Baker, who serves as a director of the Texas Heritage Museum at Hill College in Hillsboro, Texas, is author of *Lighthouses of Texas*. "Lighthouses began appearing on the Gulf coast of Texas not long after the annexation of Texas by the United States in 1845," he says. "In 1847 the U.S. Congress passed legislation for the creation of lighthouses on Galveston and Matagorda Bays. After that there was a flurry of lighthouse construction along the entire Texas coast all the way from the mouth of the Rio Grande to the mouth of the Sabine on the Louisiana state line."

Eventually lighthouses would mark dozens of key channels and threatening shoals along the Texas coast, but the state's important commercial harbors were given priority by lighthouse officials. Because of

The iron tower of the 1872 **Bolivar Point Lighthouse** near Galveston, Texas, thrusts skyward. It was here, during the hurricane of 1900, that fearful residents sought shelter, clinging to the rungs of the cast-iron spiral staircase as water from the tidal surge rose above the base of the tower.

its deep water, Galveston harbor in particular received early attention from the government Lighthouse Board.

"Galveston handled more tonnage than any port on the Texas coast," says Baker. "In some years it was one of the busiest ports in the nation."

By 1852 a cast-iron tower on Bolivar Point marked the strategic entrance to Galveston Bay and the Galveston harbor. Less than ten years after it began operation, the Bolivar Point Lighthouse became a victim and prize of war, when the Confederates pulled down the tower. Its metal was then reforged into shot and shell for use against Union troops. Construction of a replacement was delayed for several years by a lack of funding and a yellow fever epidemic that caused much of the Texas coast to be placed under quarantine. Finally completed in 1872, the new tower was 117 feet tall and held a powerful second-order Fresnel lens.

A man and woman walk along a Galveston street in the aftermath of the 1900 hurricane. This photograph illustrates the destruction left by the hurricane and flood that devastated Galveston in September of that year. Few structures remained standing after the storm, which killed thousands.

"The Bolivar Light was the only substantial human-built structure at the tip of the Bolivar peninsula, which forms one side of the entrance to Galveston harbor," Baker says.

Across from the peninsula was Galveston Island itself. By the end of the nineteenth century, the island and the city of Galveston had become a prosperous commercial center and resort community with a population of many thousands. Except for mariners who depended on its beacon for guidance, most Galveston residents of the time likely gave little thought to the tall metal tower that stood on the opposite side of the harbor entrance.

During one terrible night in 1900, however, they would look toward the lighthouse in desperation. Because of its considerable height and prominence, the Bolivar Point tower would serve as a rallying point and refuge during the murderous hurricane and flood that struck Galveston in 1900. At the height of the storm, which turned out to be the most devastating natural disaster in our nation's history, the station's powerful light offered a lone ray of hope.

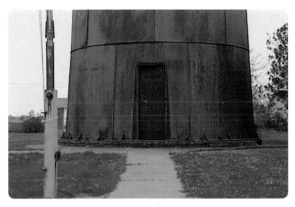

Door of Bolivar Point Lighthouse

"The Bolivar Lighthouse provided shelter both for the local people and for people who had come here on passenger trains and become stranded," says Baker. "People fled to the light station since it was the strongest structure on the tip of the peninsula. The keepers let them in, and they sat two to a rung on the spiral cast-iron staircase leading to the top of the tower."

Outside the tower thousands were drowning, but even those protected by its stout metal walls could hardly have felt secure. The entire structure rocked and shuddered in the howling wind, and flood water was pouring through the entrance driving the refugees steadily upward.

Linda McDonald

"The water rose with the tidal surge," Baker says. "It rose so high that it blocked the entrance, quite literally trapping the people inside."

Linda McDonald, a fourth-generation Galveston resident, has heard many stories about the storm from her family. "I must have been about three years old when I first heard about the 1900 storm from my grandfather," says McDonald. "It was as if he was reliving the experience."

As a child, McDonald's grandfather had witnessed the horrors of the storm firsthand. And he remembered the gracious old coastal city of Galveston as it looked before the hurricane destroyed it.

"Prior to the 1900 storm, Galveston was one of the largest cities in the state of Texas," says McDonald. "It was one of the wealthiest cities in the nation, with more millionaires per

Galveston's harbor was left a jumble of broken timbers and splintered planking after the calamitous hurricane of 1900. Once the leading harbor in Texas, Galveston never fully recovered its prominence following the disaster.

square mile than any other place in the country. Up to 95 percent of all goods and immigrants entering the state came in through the port of Galveston. There were majestic houses here, castlelike homes, and quaint Victorian cottages. There were grand buildings, such as the opera house, and historic structures, such as the state's first medical-school building. It was an era of opulence, grandeur, grace, and charm."

Those who lived in Galveston or traveled here from the mainland for a holiday by the beach felt confident, comfortable—and safe. They were completely unprepared for the calamity that struck with practically no warning on the night of September 8, 1900.

"My grandfather said that the worst thing about the storm was the sounds," says McDonald. "He said it was like a thousand demons screaming in the night. He said he heard children calling for their mothers, women screaming for help, and men begging for mercy from God. He heard soft sounds off in a distance that would get louder and louder as people floated by. The sounds would be cut off abruptly, and then he would know someone had died."

Among the most tragic stories that came out of the storm was that of an orphanage run by the Sisters of Charity of the Incarnate Word. The orphanage housed ninety-three children and ten sisters in two large dormitories near the Galveston beach.

"The sisters gathered the children in the chapel on the first floor of the girls' dormitory and tried to calm them by having them sing 'Queen of the Waves,' an old French hymn," says McDonald. "Meanwhile the waters continued to rise."

Soon waves were pounding the walls. As the dormitories were battered to pieces, each of the sisters took clothesline and tied themselves to several of the children in a desperate

186

attempt to save them. Their efforts failed. In all, ninety of the children perished along with all ten of the sisters. Only three boys survived, and they were later found clinging to the upper branches of a tree.

Says McDonald, "Every year on the anniversary of the storm, the Sisters of Charity of the Incarnate Word sing 'Queen of the Waves' to remember the children, the sisters, and all those who perished."

The hurricane and accompanying flood had many other victims—thousands, in fact. People were dying, not just in Galveston, but also on the nearby Bolivar peninsula where a floodbound passenger train left hundreds stranded. Scores of the hapless passengers struck out for the lighthouse.

"About fifty people decided to go to the lighthouse," says McDonald. "There they remained for the next fifteen hours, as the rising water drove them higher and higher up the dark tower. It must have been a terrifying experience hearing the wind howl and feeling the tower shake, but those who stayed in the lighthouse survived. The people who remained on the train did not."

The storm still haunts the people of Galveston, more than a century after it hit the city. "One time I asked my grandfather why we remember the storm," McDonald says, "why it's important to tell stories about it. He said, 'It's important to know the story of the 1900 storm because then, every night before you go to bed, you hug your family and tell them you love them. The next morning, if you're fortunate enough to wake up and still be in your house with your family around you, then you get down on your knees and thank God because it could all be gone in a night.'"

Like McDonald's grandfather, the Bolivar Point Lighthouse withstood the furor of the Galveston hurricane. It still stands, in fact, and is the oldest lighthouse in Texas. Now privately owned, it serves as a majestic reminder of a tragic and heroic past.

For more than sixty years the **Bolivar Point Lighthouse** guided vessels in and out of Galveston Bay. Deactivated in 1933, it is now privately owned.

Fifty Years from Town

Rick Pratt is the lighthouse keeper of the Aransas Pass Light Station. There have been twenty-one keepers before him, dating back to 1857, the year the lighthouse was placed in operation. "The Aransas Pass Light marks the Lydia Ann Channel, a lagoon separating two barrier islands," Pratt says.

The channel through Aransas Pass is the most direct route from the open Gulf into the port of Corpus Christi. Its beacon shining from atop a 68-foot octagonal brick tower, the lighthouse guided vessels safely through the pass. It served as an active government facility for almost a century before the shifting channel and changes in navigational technology rendered it obsolete.

"It was once important for the people of Texas to have lighthouses like this one to bring in commerce," Pratt says. "But navigation became increasingly electronic. People started using channel lights instead of large lighthouse beacons. Lighthouses became redundant, and this one just cost too much to operate."

During the 1950s the Coast Guard closed down the Aransas Pass Light Station, replacing its light with an automated beacon on the opposite side of the channel. Eventually the property was sold to private hands. The present owner is Charles Butt, who built the successful HEB grocery chain in Texas. Butt loves lighthouses, especially this one, and in Rick Pratt he found a kindred spirit.

"Sixteen years ago my wife and I took on the job of restoring the place," says Pratt. "We thought we'd be finished with that job in about three years and then move on. Well, here we are sixteen years later, still trying to finish."

The Pratts found they had taken on not only a job, but a unique lifestyle. "The biggest challenge is keeping the place running," says Pratt. "Even though we're only 2 miles from town in distance, we're fifty years from town in other ways. Out here we have to be completely self-sufficient. Our power line runs three miles across a salt marsh and then goes underneath a ship channel before it gets to us. Our telephone line takes the same route. Since we're located on a small island, everything has to come and go by boat. The pace of progress is slow, and the cost of doing business out here is high."

As it turned out, the Pratts' job involved a lot more than simply restoring the lighthouse. "This place is always trying to return to the soil. The weathering out here is very powerful, so

Lighthouse keeper Rick Pratt

Now privately owned, the **Aransas Pass Light Station** still looks much as it did 140 years ago. Although stilts keep the wooden dwellings and storage buildings above storm tides, these structures take a beating from the harsh coastal weather and require constant care. The light was discontinued during the 1950s, but has been relit as a private aide to navigation.

we just try to stay on a schedule and keep ahead of it. If you think about finishing the job, then you've already got the wrong mind-set. There are many things, major things that we've done three times during the sixteen years we've been here."

But as the Pratts see it, the work has substantial rewards. "Some of the rewards come from within," says Rick Pratt. "Once you make the adjustment, it's wonderful to live in a lighthouse. It's obviously isolated, but it's a grand isolation. We're living in a natural community that's still healthy, and we're the only people out here. Our nearest neighbors are blue herons at one time of the year and ducks at another."

Pratt says he feels a kinship with the generations of keepers who served before him. "I feel like I'm in touch with those guys from time to time, for sure," he says. "Looking at the way this place was put together, you've got to respect them. Often it will just be the way something's built. I'll be rebuilding something and I'll find in there somebody else's tracks. This is the way the last guy built it."

"There is a feeling of great peace that attends this place," Pratt says. "Who wouldn't be attracted to this job? The opportunity to come out and restore a lighthouse. How many times are you going to get that opportunity in a lifetime?"

189

The
Last Light

At the far southwestern end of the Texas coast, only 9 miles from the Mexican border, is the small town of Port Isabel. This rather sleepy and off-the-beaten-path community has a lively history. It also has a lighthouse, which has become a focusing lens, not just for Port Isabel's past, but also for its future.

"People come to Port Isabel for a variety of reasons," says Calvin Byrd. "They come for the beach, the fishing, the climate, or the proximity to Mexico. But we like to think one of the main reasons people come here is because of the people of south Texas."

Calvin Byrd

Visitors at Port Isabel Lighthouse

Port Isabel's historical resources are another important attraction. Byrd is a former mayor who made historical preservation a top priority during his time in office. The Port Isabel Lighthouse has been the centerpiece of the local preservation effort.

"My first involvement with the lighthouse was when I was growing up," Byrd says. "It was always something of a focal point for community activities, and I remember coming to Christmas caroling, fish rodeos, and all sorts of activities that were held at the lighthouse."

As mayor, Byrd became officially involved with the lighthouse. "In 1990 the state asked us to enter into a partnership with them to take over operations and maintenance of the lighthouse," says Byrd. "We saw that as a tremendous opportunity to take local control and use the lighthouse as an economic tool."

Economics was the reason the lighthouse was built in the first place. The heavy shipping traffic pouring through the nearby Brazos Santiago Pass during the mid-nineteenth century required a naviga-

Although inactive for nearly a century, the **Port Isabel Lighthouse** has been restored to prime condition by the local community. Port Isabel town officials and business owners consider it an invaluable historical resource and have made it the centerpiece of efforts to promote the area.

Rebuilt as part of a cooperative business and community lighthouse restoration project, the Port Isabel keeper's residence houses the town's Chamber of Commerce. Many in Port Isabel see the lighthouse as a "beacon of economic opportunity."

tional aide. The government responded to this need by building the Port Isabel Lighthouse, which was completed in 1852. Within half a century the coming of the railroad had curtailed shipping traffic, and the station was abandoned.

Now the lighthouse has an important new role to play. "It's a beacon of economic opportunity," says Byrd.

Port Isabel's beacon is attracting considerable positive attention. "It's something you don't see very often," says Byrd. "You can drive right by this lighthouse, within just a few hundred feet. And it's open to the public. You can experience the ambience of it and use your imagination to remember how things were or how they could have been. When you climb up in the lighthouse, it opens up your imagination tremendously."

Port Isabel has found an approach to saving its lighthouse that preserves the structure for both its past importance and its present value. "We were able to get public support for this project by promoting it, not just as historical preservation but as economic development," Byrd says. "We were able to find a practical use for this lighthouse and for the cottage. That way we were able to justify the project, and the community has responded with tremendous support."

The Port Isabel tower has been restored to its original condition, with one exception. It is missing its original Fresnel lens. The community hopes to find a replacement lens to grace the lantern room.

Although the station's old keeper's cottage vanished many years ago, an exact replica now stands not far from the tower. It serves as a visitor center and home for the Port Isabel Chamber of Commerce.

The effort put into the project has paid off. "Since the reopening of the lighthouse, we've seen a lot of new business investment in this area. It has opened up lots of opportunities to introduce people to our history, our museums, and the entire region. There are many other great things about this area—the beautiful beaches, the weather, and the fishing—but the one thing that really stands out is the lighthouse."

The **Port Isabel Lighthouse** helps to attract visitors to local museums, shops, and restaurants.

Index

Numerals in italic indicate photograph only.

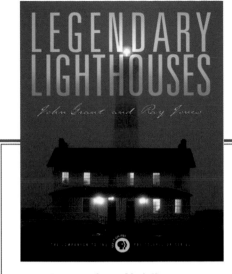

Legendary Lighthouses
JOHN GRANT and RAY JONES

The official companion volume to the six-part PBS series. Lavish color photos enhance this keepsake book.

$24.95 • 0-7627-0325-3

THE LIGHTHOUSE SERIES

Lost Lighthouses
Stories and Images of America's Vanished Lighthouses

TIM HARRISON and RAY JONES

Through dramatic photos from the collection of Lighthouse Digest editor Tim Harrison and the storytelling flair of respected author Ray Jones, Lost Lighthouses celebrates 160 of these beloved phantom towers, with stories from their "lives" and accounts of their destruction.

$17.95 • 0-7627-0443-8

Endangered Lighthouses
The Plight of 60 American Lights and the Efforts Being Made to Save Them

TIM HARRISON and RAY JONES

Over the last 100 years, many American lighthouses have been lost—destroyed by the forces of nature and those of mankind. Endangered Lighthouses tells the stories of sixty American lighthouses in peril, including their history, the dangers they face, and what efforts are being made to save them.

$19.95 • 0-7627-0815-8

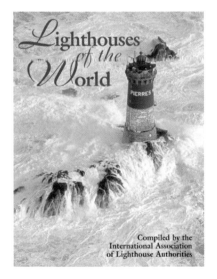

Lighthouses of the World
INTERNATIONAL ASSOCIATION OF LIGHTHOUSE AUTHORITIES

Showcasing the most unique, interesting, and important lighthouses in the world, this stunning collection of lighthouses was chosen based on architectural and historical importance.

$24.95 • 0-7627-0387-3

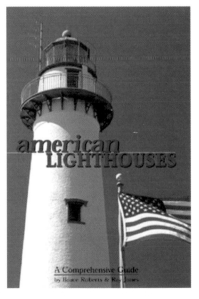

American Lighthouses
A Comprehensive Guide
BRUCE ROBERTS and RAY JONES

A stunningly illustrated, full-color archive of the history, romance, and lore of America's lighthouses. Includes complete driving directions and technical data on more than 400 lighthouses.

$21.95 • 0-7627-0324-5

The Globe Pequot Press

For a complete selection of titles on travel, history, and outdoor recreation check with your local bookseller or visit us on-line at **www.globe-pequot.com**

About the Authors

John Grant is president and executive producer of Driftwood Productions, Inc. He created and produced both *Legendary Lighthouses* series seen on PBS. He has also created, executive produced, and produced more than twenty-five hours of documentary programming for public television and cable. Prior to Driftwood Productions, Grant was senior vice president of programming at the Public Broadcasting Service (PBS). This is his third book; his other titles are *Legendary Lighthouses* and *Great American Rail Journeys* (both published by Globe Pequot). John lives with his wife, Joan, and son, Andy, in State College, Pennsylvania.

Ray Jones is a writer and publishing consultant living in Pacific Grove, California. He is the co-author of *American Lighthouses* and all eight books in The Globe Pequot Press's regional Lighthouse series as well as the co-author of *Lost Lighthouses*, *Endangered Lighthouses*, and *Legendary Lighthouses*. Ray has served as an editor for Time-Life Books, as founding editor of *Albuquerque Living* magazine, as a senior editor and writing coach at *Southern Living* magazine, and as founding publisher of Country Roads Press.

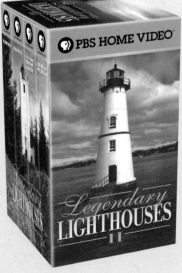